To Joyce —

Thanks!

Laurie Shoemaker

The Last Heir

A Memoir

LAURIE SHOEMAKER

Copyright © 2018 Laurie Shoemaker.

All rights reserved. No part of this book may be reproduced, stored, or transmitted by any means—whether auditory, graphic, mechanical, or electronic—without written permission of the author, except in the case of brief excerpts used in critical articles and reviews. Unauthorized reproduction of any part of this work is illegal and is punishable by law.

This book is a work of non-fiction. Unless otherwise noted, the author and the publisher make no explicit guarantees as to the accuracy of the information contained in this book and in some cases, names of people and places have been altered to protect their privacy.

Scriptures taken from the Holy Bible, New International Version®, NIV®. Copyright © 1973, 1978, 1984, 2011 by Biblica, Inc.™ Used by permission of Zondervan. All rights reserved worldwide. www.zondervan.com The "NIV" and "New International Version" are trademarks registered in the United States Patent and Trademark Office by Biblica, Inc.

ISBN: 978-1-4834-9001-4 (sc)
ISBN: 978-1-4834-9000-7 (e)

Library of Congress Control Number: 2018909689

Because of the dynamic nature of the Internet, any web addresses or links contained in this book may have changed since publication and may no longer be valid. The views expressed in this work are solely those of the author and do not necessarily reflect the views of the publisher, and the publisher hereby disclaims any responsibility for them.

Any people depicted in stock imagery provided by Getty Images are models, and such images are being used for illustrative purposes only.
Certain stock imagery © Getty Images.

Lulu Publishing Services rev. date: 09/25/2018

FOR
The sixth generation
John, Mark, Elizabeth and Erin
And
The seventh generation
Caroline, Mary Claire, Jack and Harrison

Contents

Prologue xiii

THE CHALMERS ERA

Chapter 1   Thomas and Jane 1
Chapter 2   1949 13

THE BROWN ERA

Chapter 3   Lizzie and Wilson 23

THE MOORE ERA

Chapter 4   Novice and Harrison 51
Chapter 5   Anna and Bubba 65

THE WATTERS ERA

Chapter 6   Mary Elizabeth and Joe 77
Chapter 7   The Fifties 93
Chapter 8   Coming of Age 100
Chapter 9   Christmas Gift! 113

Epilogue 119
References 125
Acknowlegdements 127

"In Dixie Land where I was born in, early on one frosty mornin'

Look away, look away, look away, Dixie land.

I wish I was in the land of cotton, old times there are not forgotten,

Look away, look away, look away, Dixie Land."

From "Dixie Land"

Written by Daniel Decatur Emmett

1859

GENERATIONS OF CHALMERS- BROWN- MOORE- WATTERS HOUSE

Generation:

1. Jane Allen Sloan Chalmers and Thomas Beasley Chalmers
2. Martha Elizabeth Chalmers Brown and Wilson Caldwell Brown
3. Novice Brown Moore and Ernest Harrison Moore
4. Mary Elizabeth Moore Watters and Joseph Skead Watters
5. Laurie Watters Shoemaker
   Mary Josephine Watters Bagley
   Sally Moore Watters Lawson
   Stanley Harrison Watters
6. John Andrew Creasy, Mark Harrison Creasy, Elizabeth Creasy Morgan, Erin Creasy Warner, Sloan Lawson Hiscock, Molly Lawson Childress, Joseph F.B. Lawson
7. Caroline Warner, Mary Claire Morgan, John P. Creasy, Harrison Creasy, Lawson Childress, Lilly Childress, Luke Childress, Sam Hiscock, George Hiscock.

Prologue

"Are you my wife"? he asked, studying me with a puzzled look. "No, Dad, remember? I'm your daughter. I'm Laurie."

I swirled the ice in the glass I held and closed my eyes. This was the fourth time in ten minutes I had answered the same question.

"Oh yeah," he replied. "I forgot. Do I have any other children?" He swallowed the last of his mostly-water cocktail and studied me with eyes dimmed by more than ten years of dementia. "Yes, Pop, I told you a minute ago. I'm the oldest, then you had two other daughters, Bunny and Sally, and then you had a son, Stan."

"Stan," he repeated. "I thought he was my brother."

"No, Pop." I yawned as I arose from my seat on the terrace, stretching stiff legs and shivering in the cool air of the Carolina autumn. "Your brother was Al. He's gone now. You're the last of your family."

In the waning light, the black birds swooped low over the expanse of lawn and found their roost under the eaves of the two hundred year old smoke house, the oldest structure on the once thriving plantation. Its tongue and groove beams leaned now, struggling to support its moss-covered roof.

Any day it could go, giving up the fight, finally succumbing as had the other ancient out-buildings on the property.

My father stood to follow me into the warmth of the kitchen. He was shuffling more now, I noticed, his shoulders slightly more hunched than the last time I had driven the ten hours to take my turn caring for him.

Inside, while I chopped vegetables, he sat staring at me, a blank expression on the still handsome face.

"Where is my wife?" he queried for the hundredth time that day.

"Remember Pop? She died about three years ago."

The headache that had begun at mid-morning pounded as I hurried to get food on the table. Only two hours left until I could tuck him in for the night. Then some peace. The end of the incessant questioning for one more day. Guiltily I clicked off the calendar days in my head. Four to go. Then, my duty done, I'd turn my car southward and escape to my life of blue sky and sunshine.

"What'd she die of?" he asked, wrinkling his brow, the pain fresh on his face.

"A really bad stroke, Dad--- remember? She lived for two days afterward. It was better that she went. She wouldn't have wanted to live in that condition."

"I guess," he said, turning his head away from me. One tear slid down the side of his cheek as the wound opened afresh. Each day it was the same.

Oh, that he would cease to ask, could be spared the truth that tore his heart anew.

We ate in silence. I attempted small talk but he concentrated only on his food, mechanically spooning each bite until his plate was clean.

Leaving the table, he walked heavily down the hall where he had come home to her from a far-a-way war, where he had held me for the first time as a new father. He moved slowly to his accustomed seat to watch the small screen in confusion until he gave up and sought the solace of the bed they had shared. I found a warmer pair of pajamas for him, saw that the toothpaste was on his brush and guided his hand to his mouth. Emerging from the bathroom, he caught my arm. With a glint in his eye, he moved to kiss me. I turned my face away, forcing the kiss to land on my cheek 'though that was not its aim. He looked hurt.

"Dad, who am I?" I asked wearily. "You're my wife", he answered. "No, Pop, I'm not. I'm your daughter. Get in bed now. I'll see you tomorrow."

With a sigh of relief, I went back to watch the television but, as usual, my mind was on him and the cruel disease that my family knew would only worsen. We sought to keep him here, living in the place he had called home for the last forty years. In their prime, my parents had forsaken their life in suburban Atlanta to return to the house that had been in Mother's family for five generations. It had been a fine life, laughably slow-paced, but good for them and they had thrived. Renovating and updating, they had created a place where their children and grandchildren would spend summers and holidays, absorbing the history and relevance of the old home place and soaking up the fresh air of the country.

Now Mother had been gone for three years, leaving the man who had worshiped her to exist in the half-life of dementia. For his four children, the job of taking care of him was out of love but exhausting. I longed for sleep but had gotten very little for the last ten days. My bed was the sofa in the den which abutted his bedroom. I could hear him if he stirred or called out. The five other bedrooms were upstairs and all of his children felt the need to be closer to him at night. I rolled out the sheeting and blankets I kept stored in the corner and plumped the pillow.

When I heard him begin his nightly rhythmical breathing, I scurried upstairs for a quick shower, slipping into my nightgown and robe. As I returned to the den, he seemed to be sleeping peacefully this night. I turned the television off and snuggled beneath my make-shift covers. The wind had picked up outside and the branches of the great oak in the side yard swayed in the light of the nearly full moon, shadowing the room with surreal images. The night was stormy somewhere not too far away and the noise would be louder in other parts of the house. This cozy room with its grass-cloth covered walls, antiques and old books on floor to ceiling shelves had become the den where family gathered, where Christmas toasts were made. Quiet evenings in front of the television were the norm, and the room was a veritable fortress with outside noises always muffled here. It had been the first home, a log cabin dating from 1835, where my ancestors came when they married. Shortly after their marriage in 1851, the industrious Thomas B. Chalmers and his new bride, Jane, would begin to add to the cabin. Soon a sturdy planter's house, with two large rooms up and two down divided by a central hall and staircase stood ready to accommodate hoped-for children.

All of us, into the sixth generation now, had known of this ancestry and tales of how the old house had come to be. Through the years, I had glanced at the portraits of my Chalmers great-great-grandparents on occasion but thought little about them except that old Thomas B. had been a handsome man.

In the dim light of the darkening moon, with the tree branches scratching the planks of the house and my father snoring lightly, I began to think of that couple and imagined them in this room. I knew that, under the modern wallboard, there was a huge fireplace, the kind log cabins required for heat and cooking long ago. Did Jane Allen Chalmers prepare meals on this hearth? What would she have served to Thomas? Fresh vegetables from a garden, no doubt, and the bounty from his hunting in the countryside. Did they dine and talk by candlelight? Did they come here after their wedding and spend their honeymoon here?

Falling asleep with Jane and Thomas on my mind, I vowed to look closer into their faces on the upstairs wall and maybe even search the ancient volumes for more about them and the life they had started here, in this very room, over a century earlier.

Morning would soon come and Dad, much like a child, would demand all my attention. But maybe when he took a nap I could begin……

THE CHALMERS ERA

Thomas Beasley Chalmers around 1880
1828-1885

Jane Allen Sloan Chalmers
1825-1890

CHAPTER ONE

Thomas and Jane

It had been a long time since Thomas Beasley Chalmers had smiled. His downtrodden expression was all he could offer as he passed his acquaintances on the street in Newberry. His focus was on his job as a clerk in the little town, the county seat of Newberry County. Grief had become his constant companion since he lost his dear wife Priscilla and his infant son Zachary.

Thomas had married Priscilla Carlisle on December 2nd, 1847 at the age of nineteen. We can assume he was farming the land his father had given him as well as working at his downtown job. At such a young age, he was the owner of six slaves, probably bequeathed to him by his father, a physician and landowner who had thirty five slaves in his care. Thomas and Priscilla lived on the property of his parents' estate and were overjoyed to learn of the expectation of a Chalmers heir the following year.

Priscilla gave birth to a son whom they named Zachary Thomas in November of 1848. But Priscilla suffered after the birth and did not fully recover. She passed from this life on December 23rd and the next day, Christmas Eve of 1848, the infant boy died as well. Thomas' father, Dr. Alexander W. Chalmers and his mother, Dorothy Beasley Chalmers, did all they could to comfort the young man but the loss affected him deeply. Only in prayer and in acceptance of God's will did Thomas eventually find solace.

Yet, Thomas was young and his broken heart would heal in time. In 1850, he proposed to Jane Allen Sloan, daughter of James Sloan and Jane Thompson Sloan. The Sloans and Chalmers were staunch Associate Reformed Presbyterians, dedicated to their Scots-Irish heritage. (Scots-Irish were originally English and Scottish Protestants who migrated to the Ulster region of northern Ireland in order to gain freedom to practice their religious beliefs. They are sometimes known as 'Ulster Scots'. The Chalmers, and Sloan families as well, were part of this sect, settling in County Antrim, Ireland. In the 1700's and 1800's, a majority of these families made their way to America, sailing to Philadelphia and settling in Pennsylvania, Virginia and the Carolinas. The Sloan and Chalmers families became prosperous landowners in what was known as the Caldwell region of Newberry County). James Sloan and his family attended Cannons Creek ARP church along with the Chalmers clan. Thomas and Jane Allen most likely knew each other from their association at church, so we can assume the wedding of the couple took place there.

The newlyweds settled on land given to them by Jane Allen's father and moved into a crude log cabin which had been owned by a man named Darby, listed in records as an overseer. The cabin was sturdily built and was most likely constructed sometime around 1830. It had a central room and an added room to the rear which was probably used as a bedroom.

"I know it is bleak, Jane," Thomas said as he helped his new bride into a chair by the open window. The heat of August had abated slightly just in time for the simple ceremony in the small country church. A gentle breeze cooled the room. The new husband had tried to prepare the cabin for his wife, making the small bed with fresh sheets. Harriet, the young house servant who would become Jane's right arm in the years to come, had pressed the sheets to a crisp finish with the heavy iron which now sat on the cold stone of the hearth. Thomas had gathered a bouquet of field flowers and placed them in a delicate vase given him by his mother. Jane noticed them immediately.

"Oh, Thomas, how lovely. Where did you find these Sweet Peas? They are my favorite. And don't fret about the cabin. I like it very much. We really need nothing more until our family…..I mean until I become…with child." The shy Jane Allen looked into the handsome face of her husband, blushing at the thought of the wedding night to come. Although older than Thomas by three years, she nevertheless felt very much the ingénue. Jane spoke in a calming, distinctive manner, tinged with the slightest brogue of her Scottish father.

The new Mr. and Mrs. Chalmers immediately set about to enlarge the structure, building around it a house made of trees cut from the property. It would be built in what has come to be known as "plantation plain", consisting of a large entrance hall with two rooms downstairs and two rooms up. The staircase faced a double front door and a veranda the length of the house gave more living space for what Thomas and Jane Allen hoped would be a large family. The kitchen was a separate building some distance away from the main house as a protection from fire.

Thomas and his strong workers somehow hauled a huge stone, over fourteen feet in length and five feet in width to be the rock which supported the foundation. Mere sand would never do. When the arduous task was complete, Thomas sat with Jane Allen by the hearth one evening.

"It's complete, my dear. I am certain that the Lord had a purpose when he said, "Everyone who hears these words and does them, I will liken him to a wise man who builds his house upon a rock. The rain came down, the floods came, and the winds blew, and beat on that house; it did not fall, for it was founded on the rock." So shall it be for us, Jane. I pray—so shall it be."

The house pleased the couple beyond their wildest expectations. The rooms were large with soaring ceilings and tall windows. Handblown panes of glass let in abundant sunshine and reflected the blue of the Carolina sky. The heart -pine-floors gave off a fresh fragrance and gleamed red-gold, polished patina. The graceful home awaited the laughter of longed-for children.

The Chalmers' first child, a daughter they christened Dorothy Priscilla, arrived on the eleventh of November, 1851. The baby thrived and had a fair beauty with blonde hair and the blue eyes of both her parents. Sadly, but not uncommon in those years, the Chalmers' next child (listed only as 'infant babe') died on the 28th of May in 1854. But a second daughter, Frances Josephine was born on the third of April 1856. Two more children followed, William Allen Chalmers on March 28th of 1860 and another son, Thomas Ebenezer Lee Chalmers on the 31st of May, 1863.

We can assume the early years of life in the Chalmers household was a merry mix of raising small children and running the plantation which consisted of cotton and food crops. Thomas became a full time planter and would have had need of the help of many slaves. Life on the farm in the 1850's must have seemed euphoric for the Chalmers family. The five hundred acres given to Jane Allen and Thomas by her father James Sloan proved fertile for the production of crops. There would have been a menagerie of animals including mules and horses for plowing, cows, chickens, pigs, and possibly goats. All this amounted to a mighty work load for the Chalmers' and required the help of both house and farm slaves. Thomas had owned 6 slaves when he married Jane and she may have brought even more into the marriage as a gift from her family. The census of 1870, after the end of Civil War, enumerated 13 workers living on the property and laboring for the Chalmers'. These were possibly former slaves who had decided to stay on after emancipation. Contrary to popular belief, not all slave owners in the South were cruel to the people they owned. Most treated them with kindness. Less than one percent of all southerners owned slaves; generally only the wealthier classes were able to purchase such people. But South Carolina held the record for slaves owned by its citizenry at 46%, inordinately high compared to the rest of the South. This was probably due to the wealthy rice plantation owners in the low country. Their vast holdings and enormous plantations required hundreds of slaves. In the upstate where the Chalmers resided, records show that Thomas' grandfather, William Chalmers, owned 49 slaves.

We do not know Thomas and Jane Allen's view of slavery but the only sect who were profoundly against the owning of slaves were the Friends (Quakers). There was an old book in the bookcase that stood in the entrance hall in the old house. Thomas had built the sturdy bookcase from trees cut on the property. It is now in the possession of Bunny Bagley. The book has since disappeared, but its title was "The Biblical Defense of Slavery." I have always wanted to study its contents but, alas, the opportunity now eludes me.

It is easy to see how the Chalmers daily workload would surely have required the help of many. The household chores would have included the washing of clothes in a tub of boiling water, the ironing of these clothes with a heavy iron kept over a stove or fire and the washing and ironing of household linens. Then there were meals to be prepared from the gleanings of farm crops, everything being grown in the earth surrounding the homestead. Fresh vegetables were served in summer along with meat from the slaughtered farm animals. Pork, and possibly beef, would have been hung in the smokehouse (which as of this writing is still standing) and cured for the winter table. Vegetables and tree-grown fruits would have been pickled and preserved. We assume the Chalmers would have shared their bounty with their slaves, so the number of mouths to feed was substantial. Thomas worked the field, planting and harvesting (largely cotton) with the aid of his slaves. A bell which hung on a pole in the backyard rang at the appropriate time for the days' work to begin, at the noon dinner hour and again at the end of the workday. This bell remained throughout the years and was a mainstay of the farm until the house was sold in 2013. As a child, I remember it still being rung by the sharecroppers and employees of the farm as they worked the still-productive fields. The ancient bell is now in Atlanta with the Bagleys.

"What are you doing my dear?" asked Thomas one October morning in 1853. His wife was digging in the soft earth a few yards from the house. Servant Harriet aided her in the planting in what appeared to be small twigs. " These are going to be lovely trees, Thomas, to give us a beautiful view in our back yard. They will yield nuts and I can use them in cooking." Jane's soft voice was filled with excitement as she labored with Harriet by her side. Her delicate skin was flushed and her blue eyes danced. Thomas took up a shovel and joined in the endeavor.

Jane Allen and Thomas planted pecan trees in the backyard and they provided shade and a lovely sight over the acreage at the back of the house. The yard consisted of sandy soil, both in the front and back, where chickens scratched and children played with their pet dogs and cats. The cool of the evening found Thomas and Jane sitting on their front porch watching the red sunset behind the pine trees and hardwood forests across their acreage. The porch at that time was rustic in nature with hewn columns supporting a slanting roof. No paint was used on the house until renovation was begun in the late 1800's by matriarch Lizzie and her husband Dr. Wilson Caldwell Brown.

The idyllic existence of the Chalmers clan began to become clouded with doubt and turmoil as the 1850's drew to a close. The question of slavery loomed in the minds of both northern and southern citizenry. The north, with its rich cities of industry, opposed the owning of individuals as property. The south could see no way to function without this labor force to plow their fields and harvest their crops. A larger issue was the topic of State's Rights. As today, while the topic is still being disputed, the South felt that the federal government had no authority to govern what they did or didn't own. The gathering clouds of secession built until the Southern states voted to secede from the Union with South Carolina being the first state to ever leave the United States. This occurred on December 20, 1860 with four more states following suit within 4 months. The Civil War officially began when Fort Sumter in the Charleston Harbor was fired upon by the Confederates on April 12th, 1861. Fort Sumter was a Union outpost occupied by Northern forces who refused to vacate the fort. Soldiers of the Confederacy bombarded the fort from the Charleston Battery with 4,000 shells until a white flag was raised by the Yankees (as they were coming to be known). No lives were lost but the intention of the South became clear. In South Carolina, and on the Chalmers farm, residents asked for God's guidance in the conflict to come.

With a sense of duty propelling his decision, Thomas joined the army of the Confederate States of America in 1861. He most likely trained in Newberry under the leadership of J.C.S. Brown who was his neighbor in the Caldwell district and would one day become his kin. It may have been Mr. Brown who recognized Thomas' skill as a rider and sharpshooter for he was recommended for service in the prestigious Stono Scouts under the command of Captain J.B.L. Walpole. A cavalry largely made up of men from the low-country around Charleston, only the best marksmen were invited to join their ranks. Thomas probably was delighted with this appointment for so many of his friends and kin were being assigned to companies out-of-state. At least he would not be far from Jane Allen and the children.

"Do not worry, Thomas", whispered Jane as they lay together in the feather bed they shared. He would leave the following day to join his assigned regiment, the Stono Scouts, and take up arms in the cause of the Confederacy. "You must follow your conscience and obey what God seems to be calling you to do. I am strong and with the help of our people, I'll be able to maintain this land until you return." Jane assured her beloved husband.

Thomas held her close. His furrowed brow was hidden by the dim lamplight. "But to take the life of another man, Jane, which will surely be my duty. The Bible……" Thomas' voice trailed off. He had struggled so with the decision to leave his dear family. Everything in his being wanted to remain with Jane on the acreage he so loved. But he had no choice. He would not seem a coward while his friends and neighbors took up their weapons. "Perhaps the time until my first furlough will go quickly."

It was customary for soldiers in the CSA to be given leave to return home at planting and harvest time. We know Thomas must have taken this leave for his son, Thomas Ebenezer Lee Chalmers (Ebbie) was born on 31 May, 1863 while Thomas was in the service of the Stono Scouts.

The skill of Walpole's Stono Scouts was tested in July of 1864 when encamped on Johns' Island to the west of Charleston. See the following account taken from the Civil War @Charleston website and written by Ted Banta, executive director of The South Carolina Battleground Preservation Trust. It tells in detail how Johns' Island and the Battle of Bloody Bridge (as it came to be known) became a vital part of the defense of Charleston and the history of the brave Stono Scouts. The water in Burden's Creek ran red with the blood of fallen soldiers on both sides. Historical accounts tell of a division of the 26th Colored Troops systematically stabbing wounded confederates with their bayonets to insure their deaths. This was only one incident of the slaughter that occurred. Your valiant grandfather, Thomas B. Chalmers, was witness to this horror.

The Palmetto State was not a major battleground for most of the war, until General William T. Sherman completed his notorious March to the Sea in the fall and winter of 1864. Up until that time, battles were usually waged when railroad lines were threatened. There were frequent skirmishes between Federal and Rebel troops and Thomas would certainly have participated in these. But on 15 January of 1865, Sherman crossed the Savannah River into South Carolina with his sights set on, first, Charleston, and then the state capital of Columbia. Charleston was referred to by the Federals as "that vipers' nest and breeding place of rebellion". Confederate troops began to assemble in greater numbers to protect the city. Thomas and the Stono Scouts were most assuredly among them.

In his book "Sherman's March through South Carolina", author John Rigdon recounts the devastation: "In Georgia, few houses were burned; here, few escaped and the country was converted into one vast bonfire. The pine forests were fired; the resin factories were fired; the public buildings and private dwellings were fired. The middle of the finest day looked black and gloomy, for a dense smoke rose on all sides clouding the very heavens—at night the tall pine trees seemed so many pillars of fire. The flames hissed and screeched, as they fed on the fat resin and dry branches, imparting to the forest a most fearful appearance.....the ruins of the homesteads of the Palmetto State will long be remembered." Residents must have been living in horror.

Back on the farm, Jane Allen was holding forth with her four children. She oversaw the acreage and tried to carry on with the production of crops and feeding the family and laborers as best she could. In the census of 1850, Thomas is listed as having 13 slaves so we assume there was at least that amount. It does seem as if he would have needed more than that number to meet the needs of his plantation. Families with husbands and fathers away at war were hit particularly hard and Soldiers' Relief Societies and churches helped as best they could.

Charleston had been heavily bombarded from some distance throughout much of the war. The Stono scouts, Thomas among them, fought valiantly and held the Confederate line. The city was in shambles and most of its citizens had fled. Sherman began his assault on Charleston as if to completely annihilate what remained but abruptly turned north and headed upcountry toward Columbia. It has been said that heavy rains in January caused his cannon and artillery to bog down in the marshy soil en route to the city. But most likely, when he saw Charleston already in ruins, he headed north with his eye set on making an example of Columbia, the capital of the state where the idea of secession first took root and, in his eyes, the seat of the rebellion.

As with his march through Georgia, Sherman's tactic was to have three branches of his troops marching at the same times in a "pitchfork" pattern, so as to cause the widest devastation possible. He referred to his foray into South Carolina as "going into the very bowels of the Confederacy." His army, well equipped and out for revenge, numbered 60,000 and cut a path from 20 to 60 miles wide. Following them were low-life vagrants called "bummers" who foraged and burned everything the soldiers did not. The word "frightened" could not begin to describe what the residents of the South must have felt at his impending approach. We know that valuables and silver were buried in the ground on most homesteads. Tales have been told of this happening in the sand around the Chalmers farm. My mother, Mary Elizabeth, recalls her brother Wilson still finding such hidden treasures when they were children. Farmers also hid their meat from the smoke house in the woods, covering it with flour and dirt to cause it to appear spoiled if uncovered by enemy soldiers.

The western-most line of Sherman's army, after helping to destroy Columbia, headed north. Maps show that it came within 12 miles of the Chalmers farm as it marched through Pomaria headed toward Winnsboro. Jane Allen would have feared the "bummers" almost as much as actual soldiers. If indeed the farm was spared, it was by the grace of God. Those left on the farm, (we don't know if Jane Allen took the children and felt safer in the town with relatives or stood firm on her property), must have been petrified. Try to imagine it: the air would have smelled like and been heavy with smoke, lights of towns and homes being burned would have been visible, especially at night. Each footstep might have been that of an enemy soldier or a dastardly bummer set on destruction. Slaves on the property may have fled or decided to help their owners defend their property. We don't know the outcome of that for Jane Allen, but her slaves would have been just as frightened as they had nowhere to go and no means of escape.

Jane Allen kept wet linens around the base of all doors and windows to lessen the smoke which drifted over the miles from the burning forests and farms.

"My eyes are stinging, mother," Dollie cried by the hearth. The family kept a nightly prayer vigil for the safety of their father. " Mine too," said William, as he began to weep. Jane Allen soothed her children with cool cloths, and encouraged them to trust in their God. But her heart was filled with fear even as she clung to the promises of scripture.

Thomas, after the victory at Bloody Bridge, marched north behind Sherman, trying desperately to stem the tide of destruction. A soldier has described that time as "marching backwards", trying to no avail to stop the juggernaut that was Sherman's war machine. But on the Yankees went, unspeakable destruction left in their wake. Finally entering North Carolina on March 9th, 1865, they faced the army of General Joseph Johnston. But for all purposes, the war was over. An account by a Federal commander describes the rebels whom he encountered as "mostly old men with grey hair, many infirm. Sickly and spent. A few young boys fought alongside them. It was a pathetic sight."

We know by that time that Rebel troops were ragged and threadbare, many with no shoes in the cold days of the winter of 1864 and 65. They were starving to the point of eating the pellets of corn dropped in the leavings of their horses and mules. The Federals made a last stand at Bentonville,

North Carolina in mid- March. Confederate troops numbered only 30,000 men while by that time Sherman's had grown to 80,000. The multi-day battle ended with the surrender of Johnston to William Sherman at Goldsboro on April 26th following the April 9th surrender of Lee to Grant at Appomattox Courthouse. General Robert E. Lee made it clear that he was surrendering only the Army of Northern Virginia to Ulysses S. Grant but, for all intents, the South was surrendered as well. The cause for which so many had given their lives ended in defeat.

Each soldier in the Confederacy was given a permission document that would insure him safe travel back to his home. This was a precious piece of paper as it guaranteed safety against those who might assume they were deserters. All horses and weapons were confiscated as well as the shoes of any soldier who still had them. So Thomas was required to walk the 316 miles over rugged terrain while barefooted. I'm sure he did so with a heavy heart as to the loss of the Confederacy but with a hopeful spirit at the reunion with his beloved family. We don't know if Jane had gotten word to him as to the condition of the farm and that of her dear children. So Thomas could only hope that somehow they had survived great destruction. His homecoming would have been one of bittersweet joy.

Hard days lay ahead for Thomas and Jane Allen Chalmers as their Confederate money was worthless. They most likely had little food and their animals would have been emaciated. But with strong Scots-Irish perseverance, they began to rebuild. Poor as they were, they still had land, a roof over their heads and family nearby to support them in the rebuilding. Devastatingly for Jane Allen, her brother Ebenezer Sloan had been killed at the battle of Knoxville. Many more relatives and friends would never come home from the bloody fields of battle. But Thomas must have taken comfort in Jane's arms, for in February 1866, their fifth child, Martha Elizabeth Chalmers was born. She grew into a strong, capable beauty who would endeavor to uphold family tradition, never leaving her homestead until her dying day and rearing her daughter to be committed to the same goal. She would become my great grandmother, Lizzie.

Thomas lived the remainder of his life on the acreage he and Jane Allen loved, dying (as family lore tells it) by the ancient smoke house on 20th May, 1885. He most likely suffered a heart attack. He was only 57 years old. Our Lizzie was nineteen.

Jane Allen lived on with her family, most assuredly with Lizzie as her companion at home. She died five years after her beloved Thomas at the age of sixty five in July of 1890. By that time, (on Valentine's Day 1889), her daughter Lizzie had married the son of Colonel (an honorary title) J.C.S. Brown, her neighbor down the road in Caldwell township. Lizzie and her new husband took up residence in the home of her birth, and together, Lizzie and Dr. Wilson Caldwell Brown would carry on the tradition begun by her parents.

As the pecan trees planted in the rear of the yard grew tall, life took on a more gentile quality as the years lengthened after the bitter war, and Lizzie and Wilson prospered. The sun still set red-gold across the fertile fields as the Browns rocked on the porch just as Jane and Thomas had done. Their story is one of a profound love and great faith. Read on.

CHAPTER TWO

1949

A memory

I was very young, only four. It was nineteen forty nine and my father had been home from the South Pacific for almost three years. We had moved to Atlanta but we visited mother's old home in the little village of Newberry on a regular basis. It was late spring and the windows were thrown open to the night air. The tall rose-colored taffeta draperies in the main room, the parlor, rustled in the breeze. In the long hallway leading from the front doors to the back of the house, I sat upon the black horsehair settee, my great grandfather beside me. Aromas of the evening meal being prepared wafted from the kitchen. I ran my hand over the curve of ebony wood carved to form the arm of the sofa. It was the sculpted image of a woman's face and hair, an art-deco piece favored by my grandmother. The wood was cool and smooth beneath my touch in contrast to the stiff firmness of the black leather seat stuffed with horsehair. I wiggled a bit as "Pappy" stared out the screened double doors. He watched the last of the scarlet sky fade to purple.

Wilson Caldwell Brown, "Pappy" as he was called, began to speak. His voice was gentle, his speech softly rolling his "r's" in a soothing drawl. "That sky reminds me when I was a boy," he told me. "I lived just down the road a piece, 'bout five miles or so. My parents had a beautiful old place then. Big front porch. I stood on that porch one night, I guess I was about yo' age, Laurie. Maybe a little oldah. My daddy was off to the war, fightin' the Yankees. But he had come on home for a spell before joinin' his regiment again. He stood out theah with me, on the porch. The sky started turnin' pink toward the south, then it got darker and redder. (Pappy pronounced it, "dahkah and reddah"). General Sherman was burnin' Columbia and we could see it all the way here. We smelled the smoke and the whole sky was lit up. Seemed like heaven was on fire. I was a scared young boy, I admit to that. My father prayed with all of us then and we just had to wait 'til we found out where the enemy was goin' to go. They were marchin' north and we thought they might come through our county."

I listened, mesmerized. My eyes grew bigger as I tried to imagine such a sky. Then we were called to supper and Pappy rose slowly, taking my hand.......

He was eighty eight then, in forty nine, but sturdy and sure in his step. We walked the length of the hall to the back porch and then out to the kitchen. The hallway seemed cavernous to me, its floor a polished, deeply hued pine. The wide boards would not be accented with a scatter rug for many years to come. The space echoed with our footsteps, our voices lost in its high-ceilinged airiness. We entered the warm kitchen as hot cornbread was placed on the table. Leftover vegetables from the garden was the fare, cooked with salt pork. Fresh squash, pole beans, rice. Deep red tomatoes served on a platter, salted and peppered, with a few spring onions. My grandfather, Dr. Harrison Moore, took his usual meal, cornbread spooned into a tall glass of cold buttermilk and dipped by teaspoonfuls into his mouth. A victim of a sensitive stomach, Granddaddy always ate little and his thin frame reflected a delicate constitution. Mama once said, "half his stomach was removed when he was younger."

My mother, his daughter, shared his minimal appetite, indulging only sparingly in the savory offerings which were grown in our fields and raised on our farm. Having given birth to my sister the year before, she ate what she wanted, which was not much, and resisted even her favorite banana pudding made that day by Carrie, the stout, black cook who had been employed by our family since my mother was a child. They called each other "John" for a reason my mother never really explained, probably some joke from the twenties. Carrie did not usually come to cook at suppertime. At night, we'd fend for ourselves, enjoying leftovers from the bounty she had prepared at the big noon meal. But she had come from her cabin down the lane "special", she said, to be with Miss Mary 'Lizbeth, her chum.

"John, you have any more a' those sweet potatoes from dinnah?" Mama asked, using her pet name. Baked sweet potatoes were allowed to cool, then peeled and sliced for a platter. A sprinkling of sugar made it one of the favorites at mealtime, a true delicacy for my father. But he would be eating alone tonight, having returned to his job in Atlanta after depositing us at the farm over the weekend.

"No'm, all they's been gone aftah today. I make some mo' tomorrah jes' for you, John," Carrie answered my mother. She gave me a sidelong look and passed by my place at the table offering the rice and gravy she carried. She was always silent when she was around me. I knew even then that she favored my newborn sister and I took it in stride. Many in the household seemed to treat me in like manner. But I was the apple of Pappy's eye and my Grandmother Novice's special girl, so I was happy. I called her Nannie and loved to curl up with her for story-time.

Pappy spoke up over the din of conversation. "I was tellin' Laurie about seein' the lights of Columbia burnin'. I've nevah forgotten that," he said, his voice trailing off.

Nannie added, "I know that, Pappy," nodding to her father. "And heah on this place they buried all the silver in the yard, Laurie, did you know that?" I shook my head. My curiosity soared and my tiny ears perked up, anticipating another tale.

"They sure did, honey. Your mama and Wilson were still findin' pieces of it even when they were little children. Remember that, Mary 'Lizbeth?"

My mother nodded as she ate a dainty forkful of hot biscuit dripping with butter. Her brother Wilson, firstborn and now living in Spartanburg, still searched the earth whenever he visited his childhood home, eagle-eyeing the fields and forests for arrowheads like the ones he'd found as a boy. He and my aunt Mattie were parents to my favorite cousin, Barbara, a chubby child four years my senior.

Laurie Shoemaker

I never forgot the fact that silver and arrowheads were buried somewhere on our land. Each summer, I dug for what seemed like hours in the sandy yard until the year it was planted in thick grass and the lawn deterred my digging with merely a kitchen spoon.

After supper, the evening passed as it did every night with the family sitting in the living room, the adults playing cards. Pappy did not indulge in card games, a holdover from his strict upbringing in the Associate Reformed Presbyterian Church. The church rules had loosened somewhat by the forties, so my grandparents, mother, aunt and uncle took turns making up a foursome of nightly players.

I loved to hear the sound of shuffling decks of cards as I played with my dolls beneath their feet. The floor had the newest covering, fashionable green and white linoleum, and was cool in summer and swept every day. Heavy smoke filled the room each night, all the family indulging in tobacco in one form or another, except for Nannie who still thought it something a woman shouldn't do even as her husband Harrison, my Granddaddy, smoked a pipe. Of course Pappy shunned the habit along with card games, sitting in his rocking chair, reading or writing or holding me on his lap. The smoke curled to the top of the room and formed a cloud of blue until someone opened a window and fresh air relieved my small lungs.

"Racing with the moon.........high across the midnight sky", Vaughn Monroe crooned from the big radio in the corner. It would be years before television made its appearance in American living rooms and radios were both entertainment and a link to the outside world. The clock on the mantle chimed and Pappy abandoned his rocking chair. As he stretched and said his goodnights, I begged to sleep in the featherbed with him and my mother acquiesced.

We entered his bedroom, a strange, dark area behind the living room with a slanting ceiling and uneven, wooden floor. Though the room had electricity, Pappy lit a single lamp beside his bed. Time stood still in this room. It was not 1949 at all, but a throwback to the turn of the century before linoleum. The ancient floor, original to the first log cabin in the early 1800's, was smooth under my feet. There was a bathroom, installed sometime in the thirties, but most bedrooms still offered a chamber pot as well. He would use it and the bathroom in cold weather but, in warm months, made his way out to the backyard to the outhouse with its Sears catalog for reading and other purposes. Sometimes I made the trip outdoors with him. Standing outside the wooden door of the rudimentary toilet while he was 'indisposed', I listened to the sounds of the farm at night. The animals in the barn shuffled softly, knowing someone was near. The crickets chirped in their unending chorus. Watchful creatures stirred in the bushes and trees. I became one with them, small and still, breathing in the cool night air. The scent of the fields and loamy, fertile furrows of earth filled my tiny being and a sense of adventure I was too young to name called to me.

This night, I was happy to be going to sleep in the downy bed with Pappy. Moving to the wash basin he kept on a stand, he directed me to brush my teeth with the little toothbrush he saved for me. He turned to face the wall and pulled long johns over his legs, only then removing his shirt and weskit, slipping a coarse nightshirt over his head. Then he knelt on the cold, hard floor beside the bed and said his evening prayers in a barely audible voice. It was my turn to say prayers when we piled beneath the quilts and I cuddled up close.

I did not know it then, but he had shared this bed with his beloved Martha Elizabeth. His "Lizzie".

Let me tell you about them............

THE BROWN ERA

Martha Elizabeth Chalmers Brown, (Lizzie) around 1888
1866-1936

Dr. Wilson Caldwell Brown, (Pappy) around 1887
1861-1951

CHAPTER THREE

Lizzie and Wilson

A memory

The afternoon was, at last, cooling off, as we sat on the patio under a clear late-summer sky. Bunny and I talked of the old times with Jesse, the last of the sharecroppers' sons, the great-grandson of slaves. He was in his seventies now but remembered the years growing up on the farm as if it were yesterday. He spoke of the generations of Browns and Moores, telling tales we had never heard.

"Dr. Brown, now, he was de man, he was de man," referring to Wilson Brown who had married Lizzie Chalmers in 1889. "He done bought every fam'ly that was workin' and livin' heah on the place, he done went out and bought 'em a car. Yessuh. Musta' been in the forties or fifties, I forget. But he bought every fam'ly a car. He was a gentleman and a great man."

Bunny and I had never heard this about our great-grandfather. But we were not surprised.

Wilson Caldwell Brown was the second son of John Christopher Sims Brown and his wife Lavinia Cannon Brown. His parents welcomed him in 1861 as he joined their firstborn son, John, born in 1857. The family resided in the countryside of Newberry County after having lost their home in the village due to a catastrophic fire which destroyed a large portion of the fledgling town. Moving to rural land owned by the Brown family for a hundred years, they built a large home with high-ceiled, airy rooms and a double veranda which spanned the front of the house. A wide, lengthy path led to a front door which was graced with glass sidelights, something talked about throughout the community. His father had been settled quite well with an inheritance from his father and now, in the census of 1860, J.C.S. Brown was listed under the profession of 'planter'. He owned many slaves and was determined, he said, to have as many children as God would grant him. He had been the only surviving child of his mother and father and lost his father at the tender age of six. Thus he longed for a large family. Lavinia, beautiful and dark-haired, agreed.

Wilson soon garnered the nickname "Wiss" and from the start, he exhibited a vigorous constitution and godly conscience. "Mother," he asked on a weekly basis, "How many more days until the Sabbath?"

His mother took delight in the sensitive four year old and said, "Just one more day, child. Then we will attend church in the afternoon after we share a hearty Sunday meal. After the service, some friends will come over to hear me practice on the harpsichord." The weekly concert kept those who attended from thinking about the dire situation they, as well as the whole nation, faced. The cause for which Wiss' father and his neighbors fought seemed all but lost.

Now, in the winter of 1865, his father had been away at war for nearly four years having left when Wilson was an infant. He had grown up watching his mother manage the vast acreage and slave holdings of the Brown family. A third son, Sims Edward, had been born the year before. Now mother to three sons, Lavinia bravely kept the homestead together as did the other women up and down the country road and in the village itself.

"Oh, good, Mother," Wiss said. "Who will be here? Are the Chalmers coming from down the road? Dolly and Fannie and William?" he spoke of his best friends and playmates.

He had become especially close to his mother in the years since his father had been gone. Wiss missed him terribly and welcomed the times when J.C.S. received a brief furlough to come to his home and oversee the planting or harvesting season. But the fighting had been so fierce last fall, Lavinia said, that his father was needed in the low country defending Fort Moultrie. It had been months since the family had seen him. His father had yet to lay eyes on his infant brother, Sims Edward.

On Sunday, all of the Browns attended church in the afternoon and, as his mother promised, gathered in the family parlor to hear her play the exquisite harpsichord. In attendance were the Chalmers and Price families. Only mothers and children gathered around to hear the ethereal music as, like Wiss' father, the men in the families were absent soldiers. Wiss thought the sound of the instrument must be akin to the music of heaven. He sat on the floor near the piano and giggled with his brother John and his friend William Chalmers. Baby Ebenezer Chalmers sat on his mother Jane Allen's lap. Dolly and Fannie Chalmers, along with the Price children, perched on the arms of delicate settees where their mothers sat in rapt attention. Wiss loved this room on these afternoons when his mother gave her recitals. It glowed with a warmth that belied the foreboding the adults felt. The children knew, too, of the impending peril they all faced, but were protected by their parents from the harsh realities of war. In the parlor, a fire which had been burning all day chased the chill of March away. A thick Persian rug kept the wood floor cozy. The room's tall windows were hung with heavy draperies and candles shed abundant light.

As the afternoon faded into dusk, the concert ended and the families said their farewells. Wiss heard his mother speak softly to Jane Chalmers as she helped her into the carriage. "I had news this morning, Jane, that there were bummers all up and down the Buncombe road. Do you have plans to take the children into town? I will leave tomorrow and take refuge with our cousins."

Young Wiss bent his ear to hear Mrs. Chalmers' reply. "I am anticipating staying as long as I dare, Lavinia," Jane Allen Chalmers replied. "Josiah and our people have assured me they are staying and will be as watchful as they can. I do so hate to leave our place to the mercy of the Yankee scoundrels and, worse, the bummers. But I won't risk endangering the children. Thank you for this reprieve, Lavinia. For a brief moment, I closed my eyes and forgot about the horror all around our dear state."

With these words, Wiss saw the neighbors depart. He knew his mother had tried to keep the news of the war from her children. But he also knew the Union soldiers were marching closer every week. An enemy general by the name of Sherman struck fear on the faces of all who mentioned his name. Secretly, young Wiss yearned to take his mother's rifle from its perch and practice shooting in the big pasture behind the house. He could help his mother, he thought, to defend the property and their gracious home that his father loved. But he knew his mother would never allow this. All he could do was kneel every night by his bedside and ask God to protect his family. He prayed fervently, as well, for the safety of his father who fought so bravely. He knelt on the wide floors of the bedroom he shared with John, whispering such a prayer, his small hands folded as he had been taught. Then he heard a noise coming from the front porch; the sound of boots and a rapping on the heavy door. He heard his mother open the door and cry out. He raced to the top of the stairs to see his father entering the long hallway.

"Father!" he ran down the stairs straight into father's arms. "You've come home! Is the war over?"

Wiss' father, who seemed so tall, took him up with one strong arm while embracing his mother with the other. He looked weary and gaunt to Wiss as the family made its way into the parlor where the embers of the fire still warmed the room. John and Wiss sat at their father's feet as he told the family the news of the war. All the children listened in rapt attention.

"I was the last one to leave Fort Moultrie," his father said. "Another soldier from Newberry, Private Perry Halfacre, and I were assigned to be the last ones out after we set the charges to blow up the remaining ammunition. It was vital that the Federals not have access to our armaments, Lavinia. We set the charges and rode horseback as far as we could, then we lit the fuse and ran the rest of the way over the bridge from Sullivan's Island to Mt.

Pleasant. It was raining bullets and shells, I tell you. My horse stumbled and I had to dismount and coax him blindfolded over the bridge and the rising water, he was so frightened. As the dynamite began to do its work, we ran like lightening. We were under Yankee fire the whole time." Lavinia put her hand to her throat and let out a tiny gasp. Wiss looked at John, then looked away. Their Father seemed so tired, and--older. Then he saw his father hesitate. J.C.S. swallowed hard and continued.

"It is by the grace of God that neither one of us was hit, although Halfacre fell when a bullet grazed his shoulder. I helped him up and together we led our horses to safety. I tell you all, my children, God was watching over us on that night. It was just two nights ago. So I was given leave to come home briefly. I must join my regiment in two days. I rode just ahead of the main column of Sherman's army, my dear wife." His Father put his arm around Wiss' mother and sighed deeply. "They will be in Columbia in no time. I want to move all of you into town to stay with our cousins. We'll begin that task tomorrow. Lavinia, don't bring a lot for the children and yourself. Just enough for a few days. We'll know after that whether there is anything left to come back to."

Young as he was, Wiss was determined to show his family how brave he could be. He would help his mother move the household into town. He would pray as he never had before. He assured himself that his courageous father and the others who fought in the Confederacy would still win the contest.

The next night, he sat on the steps of the front porch with his parents. John played silently on the wide verandah. Baby Sims Edward was in his cradle, asleep for the night. Wiss' father was saying, "Never has there been a time when one's faith is tested more than this. Our very lives, our livelihood and our futures, only God knows, Lavinia. It is up to us to trust in His care."

Suddenly, Wiss interrupted him. "Father, look. Look what a strange color the sky is." He pointed southward. The sky was exhibiting an eerie glow. There was no moon and the darkness of the night lessened with each passing moment. The boy wondered if dawn was approaching, but that didn't seem possible. "What is happening, Father?" he asked, suddenly frightened.

"It appears that the army of General Sherman has taken Columbia and is setting it ablaze. Can't say I'm surprised. Sherman hates Columbia and, sadly, our whole state, and will be more brutal than ever. God help us all," his father said, looking straight ahead at the heavens to the south.

Now the family watched the sky grow orange, then red. They smelled the smoke as the city, nearly 40 miles away, burned at the hand of the enemy. The air became acrid and Wiss felt as if he could not breathe. It looked to his young eyes as if the whole world was ablaze. Then his mother, tears filling her eyes, beckoned all the family inside. As brave as he had wished to be, he now wept too.

"We will leave at first light, Sims. Children, you must try to sleep a little. Tomorrow we will go into town and be safe. Do not fear. You will be protected." Lavinia said as she tried to calm them. The children believed her, so slept peacefully. But their father and mother watched the burning light in the sky all night. Wiss could hear them praying for their home and, indeed, their lives to be spared.

J.C.S Brown, sitting tall in the saddle, rode off at dawn to join his company as they skirted Sherman's advancing troops. "We rode at top speed", Colonel Brown said later, firing at bummers and soldiers alike as they made their way northward into North Carolina. Here, they would join the ranks of General Joseph Johnston's forces and form a final stand against the Union army.

Their mother took the family into Newberry Village and the relative safety of their cousins' homes. All in the small town waited nervously for news of the Confederate stand against the enemy at Bentonville. Finally, on April ninth, word spread like wildfire through the town that General Lee had surrendered to Ulysses Grant in Virginia.

General Joseph E. Johnston followed suit, surrendering to the victorious William T. Sherman a week later. Lavinia Brown, along with the rest of the village, sighed with relief and resignation. The cause had been lost. The Confederacy had failed. Now all slaves would be free men and women. Lavinia said she wondered how many, if any, of the people they had owned would remain to work the land and aid her in keeping the house and rearing the children. Wiss' heart broke at the thought that some who were so dear to the family would choose to leave.

Three days later, the family left the refuge of the village, returning home to find their house still standing and their vast property essentially unscathed. The small township had, mercifully, been missed by a mere 12 miles as the Yankees marched northward. Wiss' mother had no word from his father but assumed he would be given a release to return home safely over the miles he must walk to make his way home. As she drove the carriage up the long drive to the house, his mother passed a few of the slaves, knapsacks slung across their backs, walking toward the main road and freedom. She slowed the carriage and nodded to the knot of refugees. The Browns watched them go, wondering what the future held for them. Wiss would miss so many of them.

In the house, the women who had helped the Browns for years told them they would not leave. Wiss thanked God for this answer to his prayer. Most of the men, as well, would stay on to farm the land and be employed by the Brown family. They had no idea that Wiss' parents, J.C.S. and Lavinia Brown, were totally insolvent.

When Wilson's father returned, he was given the honorific of "Colonel" for his service in training his Third South Carolina Regiment and for his valor at Fort Moultrie. He would ever be known by this title. Colonel Brown gathered his family close and prayed. He, like most all the men in the county, borrowed money from the state of the South Carolina who had borrowed money from the government of the new United States.

And Wiss began, even at four years of age, to work the fields alongside his father and the remaining Negroes who had chosen to stay on the plantation. The laborers were paid meagerly at first, but shared in the increase as the land began to produce more and more cotton.

In 1867, when Wiss turned six years of age, he started his education at the Mt. Bethel Academy. His teacher said he was a bright and obedient student. This teacher, an Irishman by the name of William Brady, was fond of using the hickory stick but Wiss was quiet and studious and never felt its sting. He studied science and was a top literary student. His years spent under the teachers at Mt. Bethel prepared him well for the medical career he dreamed of pursuing.

Wilson Brown was growing into a tall, strong young man. He was devout in his faith and strong of conscience and moral turpitude. He learned early to value a good character and listened intently to his Sunday school teachers and the Reverend who preached of redemption and obedience to Christ. His family meant everything to him as he became big-brother to not only Sims Edward, but also to sisters Jane and Hannah and baby Joseph, born in 1872.

In the autumn of that year, he went off to school as usual. As a boy of twelve, he was glad to be in a different room with the older students for the first time. Younger children were taught in the large room where he had sat for the last five years. The Chalmers children were his classmates and, this year, their youngest sister Lizzie accompanied them. He greeted the first grader and was both annoyed and amused by her. She was just a child; but, after all, she was the sister of his friends, William and Ebbie. He thought of her as a bright, spunky little girl with a quick reply to every question and an opinion on everything.

In the summer of 1877, Wiss turned sixteen and prepared to leave for Due West, South Carolina and Erskine College. But the esteemed board of Mt. Bethel Academy pressed him to take on the task of refurbishing the school. His parents insisted he agree to the offer. He delayed his education to work that scorching summer on the new building. Alone, he hewed the wood and later counter-hewed the lumber until the frame for the schoolhouse was complete. As long as he lived, he would never forget the thirst he experienced. Nothing seemed to slake it, even walking into the forest and drinking long gulps of fresh spring water. He prayed for rain. Even then, he did not leave his duties, but at least he could open his mouth heavenward and seemingly be quenched.

Wiss had long days of cutting the lumber then honing it into a smooth finish. In solitude he labored, alone with his thoughts as he worked, stopping only for a lunch bundled in a basket. One day, Edgecomb Whitaker stopped by to tease him and distract him from his duty. Edgecomb would never offer to help. They were only casual acquaintances, someone with whom he was only mildly friendly. He was known around town as a scalawag and one who lacked the highest character.

"Wiss Brown," he taunted. "Look at you out here all alone in this heat. Are you getting paid for all this work? No amount of money could persuade me to work in this weather. Come on, let's sneak off to town for just this afternoon. Lots of willin' girls hanging down by the tracks I hear. Nobody'd ever know."

He was not about to be tempted to go off with Edgecomb. Wiss wouldn't leave his task and would not compromise his morals. "A man's moral conscience, Wiss, and his reputation, are really all he has in this life. One may attain wealth but that can be lost in an instant. Even a man's health is only by the grace of our Lord. Always be true to the small voice inside you and listen to its leading," his father had said on numerous occasions.

Shaking his head at the invitation, Wiss bent over the plank he was honing. His sweat fell on its fine surface in large droplets. He said to Edgecomb, "I must decline your offer and work on at this job. And Edgecomb, I pray your conscience can bear what your flesh is calling you to do. Didn't I hear that you were attending the Baptist church in town?"

With that, the surly lad scowled at him and turned tail, walking away down the road toward town. He looked back and shouted something Wiss couldn't hear. Wilson Brown would not be tempted. Yet, all afternoon, he had unclean thoughts that he had to confess constantly as he worked. Wiss turned the thoughts into prayers that God would one day bring the woman He had chosen for him. At the tender age of sixteen, he reckoned that time to be far in the future.

At the end of the summer, the muscles in his arms were as strong as steel. He was robust and fit and young ladies all over the county whispered when they caught a glimpse of him.

As he dressed for the Sabbath, his mother said, "Wiss, you are two sizes bigger than when the summer began! Your clothes will never do now for your classes at the college. I'll have some sewn for you beginning tomorrow. Soon after breakfast on Monday, go into town to the tailor and ask him to measure you." His Mother looked at him with admiration. Janie and Hannah just laughed at him and threw their corn husk dolls at his shoulders.

"Look how tall he's grown", girls in the town would comment. "And you know his father is very wealthy. The Browns own so much land out there in Caldwell Township. Their house is so large and they have hundreds of acres. He might be quite the catch. You know he's going to be a doctor__"

But Wiss always kept his heart in check and his mind set on the high ambition of becoming a physician.

At last, in the fall, he left to attend college with the hope of graduating and continuing his education at the Medical College of South Carolina. His professors said he was a fast learner and he did indeed matriculate from Erskine to the study of medicine at the venerable medical academy. Graduating in 1885, he returned home to his father's house to practice his skill, riding on horseback in the expanding county. The experience opened his eyes, sometimes in shocking ways, to the realities of the world.

"Father," he said one evening as they sat in rocking chairs on the front porch. Twilight was approaching and the rest of the younger siblings ran around the yard in an effort to catch every lightening bug that dared to flash its light. "I am just now understanding the extent to which the war maimed and marred those who fought so valiantly. Every week I am binding up wounds that are still festering today, all these years later. I am constantly amazed that many are still alive. If only there was some medicine, some elixir or poultice, which could heal the wounds and restore the health of those who are suffering. Sometimes, I feel so inadequate, I am at a loss as to how to aid them."

His father had no answer for him. As they talked on, Wiss saw in him a new respect for his son that he had previously not known. He had always known his father's love and pride, but now there was something new. An equality, so to speak, of one man to another. Wiss knew then that he had attained his majority and that he was making right decisions in his life.

The wounded soldiers of the great conflict which had ended twenty years earlier would not be the only suffering he would see as a young physician. He made his rounds as needed, treating everything from the broken arm of a schoolchild who had fallen from a tree to a heinous wound made by a scythe as the farmer who swung it missed and sliced into his leg. He attended mothers giving birth and learned to bare the heartache of babies being born too soon or the piteous ones unable to escape their mother's wombs. He saved many an infant by removing the cord wrapped around its neck.

He treated all ages, men and women alike, both black and white. By the summer of 1888, he felt older and weary. All that he had seen had taken his innocence and he viewed this world with a wizened experience beyond his years.

The joy of his life was that he was in love. As he knew God would, He had brought Wiss an ideal woman. The wonder of it had begun three years before…..

At a picnic given by his parents to celebrate his graduation from the Medical College, all the Brown's neighbors and church acquaintances were in attendance. Wiss wrestled and joked with the Chalmers brothers and paid courtesy to their sisters, Dollie and Fannie. Soon, he became aware that the youngest Chalmers girl had blossomed into someone he barely recognized. He had, of course, known Lizzie all his life. Their families were friendly and he was a frequent guest in the Chalmers home visiting his peers, William and Ebbie. He always thought of Lizzie as a silly little girl with a sharp mind and a sassy tongue who always got her way.

Lizzie Chalmers, youngest daughter of Thomas and Jane Chalmers, had always seemed, to Wiss anyway, to be favored by her parents. She grew up as the Chalmers family recovered from financial devastation after the war. Now they, like the Brown family, were prospering, their fields yielding a bounty of cotton. Wiss knew that Lizzie had known little of the bitter past, of the hard years of meager survival, of hunger and frugality. Hers was a life of promise and a modicum of luxury. America, even the post-war South, was enjoying a boon of wealth. The Industrial Revolution was sweeping the world, his father told him. Southerners were learning to live again, to taste what riches there were to be enjoyed in their thriving country. Ebbie had said that Lizzie faced the future with excitement. Her dreams could all become a reality, she just knew. Her father had told her so.

Wilson Brown studied the slender miss as he walked toward the tree under which she sat. "Well, Lizzie, you are certainly growing up," he nervously greeted the charming guest. "May I bring you some lemonade and perhaps a piece of fried chicken?" He hoped Lizzie didn't see the color heightening in his face as he spoke to the petite belle. He couldn't help noticing the curve of her small waist as she stood to greet him. He was struck by the way her hazel eyes stared at him, full of innocence, but something mischievous as well. He liked the way tendrils of her upswept, chestnut-colored hair escaped from their tortoise shell comb and curled on her neck.

"Thank you, Wiss," she answered. "Yes, but just lemonade for now. You haven't spoken to me all this year. The last time I saw you was the Sunday of Missionary Visitation at church. I guess you will be the busy doctor now. Seems like just yesterday you were riding roughshod over our place with my brothers," she laughed.

"You seem bigger, er… taller than the last time you visited our family, Lizzie," Wiss said. "You must be about….what….sixteen now?"

"Oh, Wiss, you know good and well that I just turned nineteen. You were invited to my birthday celebration, although you did not attend. I have just finished at the Female Academy in Due West. I'll be a teacher soon." Lizzie smiled up at the tall young man. He had known her for all of her years yet something neither could name passed between them. She felt her heart leap into her throat. For a moment, neither couldn't speak. Lizzie lowered her eyes, dropping her handkerchief onto the freshly swept yard surrounding the wide verandah. Wiss could tell she was nervous as she fanned herself with the hanky he promptly retrieved.

As she did so, he caught the delicate scent of lavender that she wore. When he handed her the hanky, he dared to touch her hand, ever so slightly. Wiss and Lizzie were inseparable after that, talking on into the afternoon, never leaving each other's side until the picnic ended.

As she rode off in the Chalmers' carriage, he could barely think. He retired to his room and dropped to his knees. So struck was he, that he thanked God for showing him that this was surely the woman whom he would ask to become his wife. And he had faith that she would accept him.

After the picnic to celebrate with the Brown family, Lizzie returned home that evening as if in a trance. She declined supper. "Are you ill, Lizzie?" her mother asked.

As she picked at the meal in front of her on which her mother had insisted, she announced to all who could hear, "I'm going to marry Wiss Brown, everyone. I've made up my mind. I will teach schoolchildren for a while, then we'll be married right here in the parlor. You'll see. Once I set my cap for someone, there's no changing my mind." No one in her family could argue with that.

With her excellent grades at the Due West Female Academy, she easily secured a position and began a teaching career. As autumn approached, Wiss asked permission to court her. When she agreed, he gave her a delicate set of silver condiment spoons, so tiny and elegant. Engraved into the Sterling Silver handle of the largest spoon was the message "For Elizabeth". It would be the first of a multitude of fine gifts Wilson Brown would bestow upon her. Lizzie knew she was an energetic, headstrong woman and she also knew that he would be her perfect match, should she become his wife. She thought of him constantly and the two were becoming known around both village and countryside as a 'couple.' Their parents were delighted.

In the summer of 1888, Martha Elizabeth Chalmers was twenty two and had accomplished what she had planned. She taught well in the schoolhouse, to children of elementary age. But she was growing restless and longed to take on the role of wife and mother. Would the cautious Wiss never propose? She was frustrated. She prayed often, but God seemed unable to do anything with Wiss!

Finally, as they walked in the fields behind her family's home, she said, "Wiss, some of my friends from college-Julia and Louise and Florence- have asked me to join them on the Tour in the fall. I think I will resign teaching and travel with them until next spring. Mother has agreed and it will be a wonderful opportunity for me." Wiss was silent.

They walked on, but Lizzie could tell he was disturbed. At last, he stopped in his tracks, turned to her and said, "Lizzie, you just can't go. I cannot be without you now for more than a day. How will I manage for months?"

"Well, Wilson, you will just have to," she replied, using his giving name. She referred to him in this manner whenever she grew impatient with him. Then he turned to her and she saw tears forming in his eyes.

"Lizzie," he said, "I have allowed our relationship to proceed slowly in order for you to 'grow up' a bit and for you to achieve your teaching goals. But I can wait no longer." Then he dropped to one knee on the soft grass of the pasture and took her hand. "Martha Elizabeth Chalmers, will you do me honor of becoming my wife? I have loved you since that day at the picnic at my house, and I know you love me too."

She clasped his broad shoulders and helped him to his feet. She boldly leaned to kiss him and whispered, "Of course I will. I have been waiting for three years for you to ask." Then Wiss wrapped her in his embrace and held her for the longest time. They walked slowly back to the house.

Then, to her amazement, she began to babble. "Oh, now, I have already picked a date, Wiss. It will be Valentines' Day of the year to come. Of course it will be here in the parlor and......"

Wiss threw his head back in laughter. "Oh my spunky little Lizzie. You, as usual, are way ahead of me aren't you?" He laughed at her and she pretended to pout.

"Don't tease me, Wiss. A girl always dreams and plans for these things. I set my sights on you at that picnic and asked God for you and He has done it. I always knew He would. I've got it all planned......" And she rambled on for the longest time. The winter passed quickly as they were feted by a multitude of friends of both families. There were teas and bridal showers and dances filling up that cold winter of 1888. As February neared, the weather was slightly warmer and the tiniest spring flowers poked their tender shoots up in the rich soil of the Chalmers yard. Valentine's Day of 1889 dawned clear and chilly, but the house was bustling with activity.

Lizzie's sisters said she never looked more beautiful. Upstairs in the house her father had built in 1851, she giggled with her sisters, Dollie and Fannie. They were dressed in pale blue and carried nosegays of blue Sweet William. Her Mother had somehow found the delicate flowers and ordered them for Lizzie, her last daughter to wed.

The gaiety of the occasion was marred only by the absence of her dear father, Thomas.

The month before she was to graduate from the Due West Female Academy, her Father died suddenly of a massive heart attack at the age of fifty seven. He had walked one morning over the acres of his beloved farm, stopping to assess the supply of meat hanging in the ancient smokehouse. Lizzie saw him close the old door tightly, and knew he was assured that there was an ample supply of pork to last the summer. As he turned to join the family back inside the house, Lizzie heard him cry out as he clutched at his chest. Falling to the ground on the soft soil he had loved so well, he was praying when Jane Allen and Lizzie reached him. Accepting that this would be his last hour on earth, he faded from consciousness. He looked at his dear

Jane and whispered the names of the children she had borne him. His last word was his daughter's name- "Elizabeth."

Now, her father having been gone for four years, Lizzie was the daughter he had always referred to as his "whip–smart young lady." She was marrying the man on whom she had set her sights, the man she knew her father would have approved.

It was St. Valentine's Day, 1889. Lizzie felt resplendent in a two-piece golden silk gown. She wore a matching jacket with a high neck trimmed in lace to keep her warm. Her tiny waist was accentuated by the slightest hint of a bustle, a 'must-have' for all fashionable young ladies in the 1880's. A small length of fabric represented a train which elongated the back of the skirt. In England, Queen Victoria had set the style. Lizzie thought her own gown the perfect example of the new haute couture.

"Oh Lizzie! The house is so full downstairs! They are all waiting for you. Mother is looking up the stairs. It must be time for you to go down," Fannie said, tucking a small lock of Lizzie's hair under her short veil. Then, peeking around the top of the bannister, she continued, "There…now I can see Wiss. Oh, Lizzie, he is so handsome. And he loves you so much. Be mindful or he will spoil you into becoming someone we don't like."

"Not to worry, Fannie," she said. "He does love me so very much, but I respect him and we make a good match. I know it was meant to be. I knew it that day at the Brown's picnic four years ago."

With that, she slowly descended the stairs into the hallway that led to the parlor. Her brother William waited at the last step to extend his arm and escort her to the groom. She thought of her dear father and how he had looked forward to this day. She walked slowly toward the fireplace which glowed with a day-long fire as did all the fireplaces in the house. The mantle was adorned with holly and magnolia leaves, red berries and roses scattered in remembrance of Valentine's Day. Lizzie carried a delicate bouquet of white Narcissus, the first of the spring flowers to come. A violin was played softly by brother Ebenezer. The Brown and Chalmers families, along with faithful friends, filled the house and regarded the handsome couple with admiration. To be sure, all would have to say, they were a striking pair. Wiss was elegant in his black suit and high-necked, starched shirt and white weskit. He wore his grandfather's brass stud set and cufflinks. He seemed so tall as he stood by her side. She felt loved and safe with this godly, honorable man.

The ceremony having ended a little past noon, the new Dr. and Mrs. Wilson Caldwell Brown departed in a carriage to the train station. They would spend a week in Charleston for their honeymoon. Upon their return, they would reside in the Chalmers family home with Lizzie's mother Jane.

There had never been any doubt that the couple would dwell in the old home Thomas Chalmers had built. Lizzie's siblings had moved on, making lives of their own. Except for her sister, Fannie. Always painfully shy, Fannie was neither gifted nor beautiful. Yet, her sweet temperament made up for her shortcomings. She lived still with her mother after her father's death. Fannie felt an obligation to care for her widowed mother and sister and to carry on the ownership of the Chalmers' plantation. Lizzie remembered well her father's words, "This land and this house, Lizzie, is our heritage. It is what we in the South fought for. We must thank God for it and guard it so that it might be passed on to future generations. Of all my children, dear daughter, you know of which I speak. You have the fortitude to keep up this legacy, Lizzie."

Wiss understood his wife's wish to reside in her family home and her determination to live on in the life she had always known. He honored her desire to carry out her father's wishes. Above all, he was deeply in love with Martha Elizabeth and thought her a fascinating, strong woman. He vowed to keep her loving him in return. Life in the lovely old home would not be as grand as the one in which he grew up down the road at the Brown family plantation. But it would be a prosperous life and a happy home, he assured his wife.

Returning from their brief honeymoon in Charleston, Wiss set about to establish his practice of medicine throughout the county. Lizzie took over as mistress of the household, watching over her aging mother with care.

Her spinster sister Fannie helped with the kitchen and tutored students on a weekly basis. To her surprise, a few weeks after returning from her Charleston honeymoon, Lizzie found that she was to have a child.

"Wiss," she said in the privacy of their bedroom with its slanting wood floor, "I visited Doctor Martin today and we are going to be parents. I cannot believe it has happened so fast. How do you feel about this piece of news?" she teased.

"I am not surprised my dear," Wiss said. "I believe children to be a gift. God has given me you for my wife and is continuing the blessing by giving us a child. I'm so happy, Lizzie."

Lizzie had longed to give her mother a grandchild, hoping it would restore the woman's health. Jane was nearing her seventieth year and the entire family was distraught at her condition.

Since losing her husband five years before, Jane Allen Chalmers had become a shadow of the woman she once was. Her always-quiet demeanor grew into solitude. She spoke only occasionally. She declined taking sustenance and gave up walking in the garden as she had done her entire life. She stared for long hours out of the hand-blown glass windows that Thomas had installed nearly forty years before. The birth of her grandchild cheered her somewhat, but within a few short weeks, she took to her bed, never to leave it. When she died in 1890, Fannie and Lizzie were desolate. Most said their mother had died of a broken heart.

After her mother's death, Lizzie made an effort to carry on as usual. The old family servant Harriet still lived on the place and was now a paid worker. An accomplished cook, old black Aunt Rose, assisted Bessie in the kitchen. Mary remained a house laborer and the sons of Josiah and Obie lived in the same cabins as their ancestors and were invaluable help in farming the land.

Wiss employed an overseer to direct the day to day farm operations while he continued his medical practice, but found he was needed much of the time in his role as joint land-owner with his wife. He loved the soil and farming. He loved riding over the acres on his American Saddlebred, Ranger. Thomas' old horse, Gabriel, had survived the battlefield with his master and still fed each day in the pasture. Wiss confided in his wife of his love of the vast acreage, saying it had a 'spirit' about it and a 'presence'. The land whispered to the young doctor, filling him with awe, touching the tender soul within him. He told her he found that he was nearest to God as he rode over the acres, stopping to pray by a small stream or outcropping of rocks. Within a few short months after their marriage, he had come to love the plantation, its haunting fields and abundant forests, as much as Lizzie did.

When a daughter was born to the Browns in December of 1889, Lizzie wanted a name for the baby that was unusual and clever. "We shall call her Novice," the new mother announced. "Something entirely different; it means "new", of course. She is our new creation. A new generation to carry on in this house. What do you think, Wiss?"

"I think it is very different, very inventive, my dear," her amused husband answered. "Will she have a middle name? Perhaps "Jane" or "Lavinia" after her grandmothers?" He was in awe of Lizzie's modern sense of style, even as it pertained to a name for their daughter.

"No, I think not. I think 'Novice' is definitely so different it requires no second name. She is so beautiful, Wiss. She looks like she will have your brown eyes." Then she put the baby to breast in an effort to stop her crying.

The infant seemed to be fretful most of the time and, by spring, Lizzie's nerves were on edge. Wiss hired an extra nurse to comfort the child at night so he could get his needed rest. Only when he held his daughter did she seem content and the crying lessened.

Wiss delighted in his child and said he loved her more than he could ever express. He found being at home with his family, seeing to the farm and its production, to be his true happiness. He thought himself blessed and a more contented man he could not imagine meeting. To his delight, Lizzie presented him with a son in 1892, naming him Thomas Chalmers Brown. The baby's three-year-old sister promptly dubbed him "Bubba".

The household was a happy, bustling hive of activity with father, mother, aunt, son and daughter living in the ancestral home. Lizzie became the matriarch and overseer of cooks and maids, several dogs and assorted outdoor cats. Visitors came and went on a regular basis. Cousins, aunts and uncles of the large Brown and Chalmers families were frequent guests.

"Your energy and zest for life fills every room and overflows into the outside yard around our house, Lizzie," Wiss said to her one day. She consulted a landscaper, decided she could do as well, and created beds for abundant flowers and shrubbery. With the help of tireless young Moses, the grandson of slaves, she installed a lawn around the front of the house and added a walkway to the front door. Wiss planted a vast garden behind the house and grew melons, corn, cabbage, tomatoes, beans and strawberries. The bounty the garden produced was canned and preserved in glass jars and saved in an underground glass cool-house.

When Wiss developed a gastric disorder in 1893, he agonized over the decision to continue his practice as a physician and the burden of overseeing the plantation as well. It seemed, at times, too great a task even for the accomplished Wilson Brown. So, at his wife's urging, he abandoned the field of medicine and became a full-time gentleman farmer. On the five hundred acres they owned as well as acreage from the Brown family holdings, he was a prolific producer of cotton and food crops for the county.

Wiss built, largely with his own hands, a gin to process his own cotton as well as that of any who paid the price to have their own crop ginned. The Sloan-Chalmers-Brown farm grew in reputation and in monetary gain. Lizzie knew her parents would have been pleased.

Then, ever the astute observant of everything current and modern, she began to renovate the home, adding a kitchen to the back of the house and expanding the veranda. She commissioned gracefully-turned Victorian columns to be built the length of the porch. A large dining room was added to adjoin the parlor. She instructed carpenters to cut a pass-through window that opened to the back porch. Here, the hot food from the kitchen could be handed through the open window into the dining room. The busy household continued to be blessed by health and good fortune. But in the winter of 1894, tragedy struck.

Lizzie's dear sister Dollie, eldest of the siblings, had suffered with a high fever for days. Her husband John Thompson was frantic. His beautiful blond wife had never been ill and their three children cried for their mother's attention. Dollie became so desperately ill that Wiss and Lizzie offered to take her into their home in order to nurse her back to health. They confined her to an upstairs bedroom, moving their young children, Novice and Bubba, downstairs and instructing them to never go near the sick room.

In no time, Dollie was delirious with fever and a red rash appeared on her abdomen. The same day the rash began, sister Fannie also fell ill. She joined her sister in the upstairs bedroom. Lizzie summoned the doctor from town and Wiss ministered to the sisters day and night. He kept cool cloths on their foreheads and Lizzie bathed them in cold water in an attempt to bring down their fevers.

"I fear it to be measles," Wiss said on the fourth morning after Dollie arrived. "Keep her children in town. I know they are crying to see their mother, but we cannot risk it. This is a rampant, contagious disease, Lizzie. Better move our own Novice and Bubba into town. They can stay with my sister Janie or Hannah would love to have them. And I forbid you to go into the sick room anymore." Wiss knew by the look on Lizzie's face that his warning had fallen on deaf ears.

Wiss and Lizzie continued to put their own health at risk but promptly moved the children into town to the safety of relatives' homes. They prayed over Dollie and Fannie as the sisters suffered together in the bedroom. Lizzie tried to get them to take sips of water and changed the linens several times a day as their fevers rose and broke in endless sweating. On the sixth day, Dollie lapsed into a coma. Fannie, always frail, moaned in agony out of fear. Then she too succumbed to unconsciousness. By week's end, the two had died of the dreaded disease.

The Browns, individually and as a couple, were inconsolable. They were faced with the task of imparting the news to the Thomspon family- husband John, and children Tommy, Josephine and Kate. They held a wake for the two sisters and Wiss read from the Psalms at the burial. Back home on the farm, Lizzie wiped away her tears and straightened her shoulders with resolve.

At the news of his wife's death, John Thompson collapsed. He refused to speak for months and had nothing to do with his children. He was hospitalized briefly in a sanitarium. It was rumored that he had suffered a total nervous collapse. When he returned to his home, he was unable to work, spending months at a time in and out of the sanitarium.

The Browns tried to be sympathetic, but had no patience with John's weakness. Lizzie pitied the children who were being shuffled from relative to relative. They had sustained the loss of their mother and now their father seemed incapable of caring for them. And so, she set out to find a solution.

"Wiss, dear husband. Thank you for all you have done during this dreadful time", Lizzie said as they sat by the fire. "You have been my rock and my fortress. But I have one great request of you. Take your time in giving me your answer as this is no light decision. It is my wish to now take Dollie and John's children to live here with us and have them grow up with our own family. We have the room and Kate and Novice are already like sisters. But don't decide now. It is a great responsibility, I know." She patted her husband's hand and rose to leave him alone with his thoughts.

Wiss needed no time to answer her. He did not hesitate. "Of course they will live here with us. There is no need to even ask, Lizzie. I'll tell Moses to bring the carriage and we will collect them this very afternoon. Moses and Zachariah can fetch the rest of what they need in the coming week." Wiss' love for his wife knew no bounds. Too, he loved the motherless Thompson children as his own. He would raise them, provide for them and shelter them in the spacious home Thomas Chalmers had built.

And so the household grew to now include five children. After the shock of their mother's death, the Thompson children came to love the life Wiss and

Lizzie provided. They grew in stature and in spirit, receiving an excellent education at Mt. Bethel Academy. Kate and Josephine aspired to attend college with Novice. When Tommy, the Thompson's only son, became needful of his father, he chose to spend the majority of his time with John Thompson. He cared for the pathetic man until John recovered from his loss and indeed met and married a second wife. Tommy grew into a handsome, astute business man, moving with his bride Daisy to Columbia. The cousins, Novice, Kate and Jo, until their dying day, remained as close as if they were born of the same parentage.

In the summer of 1908, young Novice was the apple of her father's eye. Wiss doted on his daughter to the consternation of son Chalmers, two years his sister's junior. "Bubba" resented the accomplishments of his sibling and coveted the attention shown to her. He, of all the children living under the Brown's roof, displayed belligerence and a surly attitude. He was never happy, it seemed, to his longsuffering father. He was sent away to various schools but was always asked not to return. He was a source of constant prayer for his parents and they fretted over their wayward child.

To her great frustration, in the fall of that year Lizzie began to experience debilitating headaches.

"Just let me rest for a few minutes, Wiss," she would say. "Novice, if you could just bring me a cool cloth and some ice-- that will be the answer." Her health now seemed fragile where once it had been so strong. She had always been a pillar of strength and exuberance to all the family. Wiss was concerned and aided his cherished Lizzie as best he could, prescribing powders and potions to ease her pain. Novice, Kate and Josephine took over the running of the house. Lizzie was furious at her own infirmity, powerless at last over something she could not control. But she soldiered on, striving to remain the resilient matriarch she had always been.

Her agony would continue for years to come. Doctors were at a loss to find a cause. Lizzie's ill health began to affect everyone in the household, most of all her nurturing nineteen-year-old daughter, Novice.

Novice Brown cared for her mother and father with inordinate devotion.

She would nurse her mother through an illness which would cause her to lose the sight of an eye requiring the beauteous Lizzie to wear an eye patch after its removal. She suffered on, quite possibly with cancer. Novice was inconsolable when Lizzie departed this life in 1936, leaving behind her dear Wiss, the devoted husband who had so adored her. Novice was left to step into the position of matriarch and overseer of the family home as well as wife to Dr. Harrison Moore and mother of two children, Wilson and Mary Elizabeth.

Let's explore the life of this fragile, brown-eyed belle, my grandmother.

THE MOORE ERA

Novice Brown Moore (Nannie), around 1910
1889-1953

Dr. Ernest Harrison Moore (Granddaddy), around 1910
1880-1962

CHAPTER FOUR

Novice and Harrison

A Memory

I peeked over the edge of the coffin to see her. She looked so pretty. Surely she would just wake up and tell us all it had been a mistake. She would laugh at the joke and then join her friends and family at the party. It was supposed to be a wake, but really, it turned into a party - albeit in hushed echoes of jubilation. Surely she would hug me close again and I would smell the Evening in Paris on the hanky she kept tucked into her comforting bosom.

"She just can't stay away," cousin Vinnie Kate said, watching me as I came back again and again for another look at my 'Nannie'. My mother Mary Elizabeth could not stop weeping. Earlier that week, in Atlanta, I heard her early morning cry as my father broke the news that her dear mother Novice had been found dead in her own bed. The cook, Janie Mae, came to see why her employer had not appeared in the kitchen as was her usual morning custom. Novice was not breathing, so Janie Mae summoned Nannie's brother, Bubba. When Bubba called our home in Atlanta with news, his terse message to my father was "tell Mary Elizabeth her mother's dead." Mother fell to pieces and never stopped the tears even after throwing herself into planning all the myriad details of the quintessential Southern funeral. There had been a casket to choose, flowers to order, food to be brought in (although she must have known the family would be inundated in both as was tradition in the little town). Indeed, I decided I loved funerals for the euphoric scents they brought to the house. I have loved them for that reason ever since.

Nannie was laid to rest beside her mother Lizzie and father Wilson Brown in the old cemetery. I was but eight years old, yet she will remain the loving grandmother of my childhood, with her luxurious big Lincoln and its stiff-fuzzy seats, her corsets with the bones that curiously made her look broader rather than holding her in. She taught me to pray and her well-marked Bible brings comfort to this day that she had a peace about where she would reside after this earthly life.

My grandfather, distant and stoic, pressed on without her. I don't remember a tear at the funeral or later, but surely there must have been some. I do remember my mother's endless sadness and that we remained in Newberry all the following summer with Mother looking after her widowed father and overseeing the house, receiving consoling visitors and remembering Nannie. There were arrangements to be made, and it was decided that Granddaddy's sister Louise would come to live with him and run his household. So that was the way it was from 1953 until his death ten years later, but we visited even more than when Nannie was alive so mother could check on her father.

Another memory………

In 2008, after both my parents had passed on, a few years went by while we decided what to do with the home and lands the four of us children had inherited. It was a wrenching decision for we knew it had always been our mother's wish that "Greenfield Farm", as she had named it, never leave the family. Yet all of us had fashioned lives apart from the tiny town and a country lifestyle. We lived in cities far from the small community in South Carolina. Only second sister Bunny had any plausible ability to move there and carry on the tradition, but her heart was not in it. She, more than any of us, felt a responsibility to mother's wishes. The stress of the decision weighed heavily upon her. So, finally, it was decided to begin the dismantling of the house after nearly two hundred years. The task was daunting and heartbreaking. Memories flooded us as we worked over the five weeks it took to clean out and distribute the cherished heirlooms, books, papers and memorabilia.

One afternoon, we opened a closet that was rarely, if ever, looked into. The wedding dresses belonging to Lizzie Chalmers Brown and Novice Brown

Moore, our grandmother and great-grandmother, hung wrapped in protective paper. We uncovered them and drew straws as to who would keep them. I was the lucky winner of Lizzies' gold silk, worn in 1889, but the 1912, delicate tulle with its silvered edges and pearls began to fall apart as soon as we touched it. Because it was coming apart in our hands, we decide to "share" it, parting out the skirt and shawl with its glistening fringe and painstakingly sewn pearls. A beautiful silk rose etched in silver and attached at the neckline was the prize piece.

I know now that Novice Brown Moore, my "Nannie", was so like her dress. Time had not been kind to her. Like the dress she chose when she married Dr. Harrison Moore, she proved to be at times sparkling and resplendent, then fragile and delicate—and easily dismantled.

....

1889

"We will call her Novice—she is a new creation," announced Lizzie Brown. Her new daughter was the apple of her father's eye and inherited his warm, kindly brown eyes and her mother's petite stature. From the start Novice set out to be the daughter her mother expected her to be. She was an astute student, obedient to her parents, devout believer in the faith, and feted belle in the small town of her birth. There was little to do otherwise, brought up with cooks, household help and workers on the lush acreage owned by the Browns. She learned to play the piano and sew, attended teas and luncheons and never missed a Sabbath at church. Novice was joined by a brother, Chalmers or "Bubba" as the family called him, and found much happiness when her cousins Kate and Josephine were taken in by her parents after the death of their mother, Dollie.

When Novice graduated with honors from Mt. Bethel Academy, she followed in her mother Lizzie's footsteps, attending the Due West Female Academy and earning a degree in education. She immediately found a position teaching in a one-room schoolhouse in the Silverstreet section of Newberry, some distance from her family home.

"I just don't like you being that far away, Novice. You must find a different position closer to home—perhaps even in town. Even that would be better than all the way out there." Lizzie pronounced it "theah" in her soft drawl.

"Mother, I'll be alright. There's a boarding house near the school where I will have a room—it takes only young ladies. I can come straight home on Friday afternoons and have all weekend here with you and Papa."

"Lizzie, she must leave the nest for just a little while. Let her try it. She'll be back in no time if it's not to her liking." Wiss Brown hated to see his daughter leave the safety and comfort of the farm, but knew this was now a different world where young ladies were 'testing their wings' and building their own futures. His protective wife Lizzie finally acquiesced to her daughter's plan.

Novice loved the teaching job but found at once an emptiness and longing for her home and family. She soldiered on, never missing a weekend, holiday or summer when she was not under their roof.

One evening in the first year of her life in Silverstreet, Novice was summoned downstairs by a gaggle of girls gathered in the parlor. "Novice, come down here and have some tea and cake. There are some young gentlemen that Mary knows and she needs help entertaining them." Novice descended the stairs and entered the large parlor. Dressed in a white shirt waist and dark skirt, as was the almost universal uniform for young ladies of the day, Novice was the picture of comely womanhood. Petite but curvaceous, she was possessed of a clear complexion, deep brown eyes with thick lashes and luxurious, chestnut hair.

The air in the room hung heavy with the late spring heat. A bowl of gardenias imbued the house with a heady perfume. As Novice sipped her iced tea, a thin young man with piercing blue eyes introduced himself. Harrison Moore said he was from Spartanburg and had just graduated from the Medical College of South Carolina in Charleston. He was beginning a practice and, like Novice, lived in Silverstreet.

"Oh, my father is a doctor and graduated from the same," the pretty young teacher replied. "But he has stepped back from medicine due to health issues and to oversee our crops."

"I believe I heard you raise cotton?" asked the shy doctor. He had obviously been given information about Novice and her family.

"Yes, lots of it," a nervous Novice answered. The dainty teacher felt a trickle of perspiration down her neck and knew her hair, upswept in its bun, would be springing curls even as she spoke. The young man was slight of build but possessed of a fine-boned face and aquiline Scottish nose. His character expressed itself in his speech and manner. He stared at her in a kind, appreciative way.

When they parted, Novice knew she would be courted by Dr. Harrison Moore of Spartanburg. She had disturbing feelings about this. Would it interfere with her time at home with her dear parents? It would be such a long way for him to travel to the farm to spend time with her.

Novice needn't have fretted. As of their meeting, the doctor was smitten. He thought of nothing but the beautiful teacher with the lively brown eyes from the moment they met. He immediately began to give her a rush of attention.

"He's trying to sweep you off your feet," Lizzie told her daughter. "He seems nice enough, but be cautious, Novice. Get to know him. What are his plans? Does he go to church? What kind of family does he come from?" Lizzie was full of curiosity about the young man who seemed so taken with her daughter.

Harrison Moore traveled the miles to the Brown farm as if on wings. He rode horseback, his daily transport in his role as country doctor, or sometimes an old motorbike borrowed from a friend. He sat by Novice's side on the verandah on summer evenings and attended church, picnics and any other function she chose, just to be by her side. He shared meals at the Brown table and found he had much in common with the kindly Dr. Wilson Brown. Novice's mother was more distant and seemed to be sizing him up at every occasion.

The slender young doctor was full of stories about his large family back in Spartanburg. Eldest of the surviving twelve children of Levi and Mary Ellen Harrison Moore (there had been 14 but 2 died as children), he was working to help his next oldest brother to attend college. Indeed, this was the family commitment-- that each sibling helped to pay for the education of the next in line. The family seemed solid to the discerning Lizzie, apart from the fact that they were of the Methodist faith. But she saw the love Harrison had for her daughter and his determination to have her. Would he marry her and take her far away?

Months of courtship ensued until talk of marriage was the foremost topic. One evening in 1911 as Novice waited for Harrison, she knew she was to be the recipient of a surprise but, in reality, it wasn't much of one. Word had already reached her that Dr. Moore had purchased an automobile. The poor fellow, she thought. At last the days of calling on his patients on horseback would be over. His practice was improving. In the beginning, before the family owned a telephone, he wrote to her of one, perhaps two patients a day. Now he was becoming better known and people knew him to be a serious practitioner, one who possessed a gift for diagnostics. His manner was more studious and a bit dry, but he had a keen knowledge of anatomy and could cure most any ailment that plagued the country people who were the majority of his patients. The quintessential country doctor, he set broken bones and stitched cuts, applied poultices and balms for rashes and gout and boils, delivered babies and heard the death rattle of the aged, some of whom he could save and some he could not. He treated both Negroes and whites, something few in the small medical community could claim.

Dr. Moore was indeed the owner of a new 1912 Maxwell and he couldn't wait to show it to Novice. As he drove through the little town on his way to retrieve the comely Novice for the afternoon, he had one stop to make. He pulled into the bare yard of a dilapidated house at the end of a rutted dirt road. This patient was in the last stages of a pregnancy she should not be suffering, a victim of a lustful husband who drank and was rarely in residence to help raise the three offspring he'd already fathered. His wife was barely out of childhood herself. "Couldn't be more'n seventeen", he'd told Novice. He would look in on the woman and her children, then race toward the date with his beloved. And race he would.

"This is the day", he told himself. He would take Miss Brown to the picnic in his glorious new vehicle and stop on the way home in a spot he had in mind. He would pull from his pocket a diamond, one worthy of such a woman, set in platinum with smaller diamonds trailing down the band. She would be amazed and delighted, he just knew. Surely she would then answer 'yes' to his pleadings for her to be his wife. Yes, this was certainly the day.

The roof of his patient's house still dripped morning rain although the sun had been blazing for hours. The little cabin was encased in the gloom of shadowing pines which kept out the light except in small rays that splintered through the branches. There was a dank, musty smell outside as well as in. The ragged children played with sticks on the front porch as an old hound licked sores on his legs nearby. The boys and their sister, their dirty faces breaking into grins when they saw the doctor, looked up in hopeful greeting. Dr. Moore always left them a dime each every time he came to see their mother. "Mama's in 'ere, doc," they said, nodding toward the door. "She ain't feelin' too good today. You got us sumthin'?" one of them asked, looking hopefully at Harrison's pockets.

Harrison nodded and walked past them. He would distribute the dimes when he was finished and not before. It was his custom. Entering the darkened cabin, he saw Nelda on the bed, her legs drawn up. "You alright, Miz Price?" Harrison spoke to the woman quietly in case she was sleeping.

"I'm not....so...." her voice trailed off. She appeared feverish to the doctor and a little dazed. She turned to sit up but Harrison told her to stay still. He took her pulse and listened to her heartbeat. Rising, he rinsed a tin cup and filled it with water from a nearby bucket. He placed the cup to Nelda's lips and made sure she drank it all. Then he moved the stethoscope to her belly. "I'm just gonna see if I can hear the baby", he said gently. He listened intently as her chest rose and fell in labored breath.

Nelda Price was thin except for her pregnancy. Listening for a fetal heartbeat, Harrison saw the frailty of her arms and legs. Long legs and pretty hands. She was only seventeen. Her hair was thick and dark and her lidded eyes a chocolate brown. Her mouth was full as she struggled to breathe with the baby pressing high up on her ribcage. Not for the first time, Harrison felt an embarrassing desire flare in his blood. When his patients were so young, some so pretty----.

"Not long now; maybe a week, two at the most. I'll be stopping by regularly now. Is Mr. Price around?" He knew the answer.

"No, suh, he ain't showed up for the past few days. I been tryin' to get up and see to the kids, but my back and legs give out so easy. He be here direckly, I hope. If you see him down in the town, kindly tell him I need him, if you will doc."

"I will do that, Nelda....ah, Miz Price." Harrison never let himself be too familiar.

He pulled a dirty blanket over his patient and tucked it around a thin, smooth shoulder. Walking to his car, he remembered the dimes and deposited one in each little hand. "Now, you be good and help your mama, you hear?"

Driving back to the main road through the thicket of pine and oak, Harrison thought of the beauty of his young patient and knew what lay ahead for her. The hard years would not be kind to her and she would be old before her time. He could not keep from thinking about the long legs with their smooth skin and the way Nelda's hair fell across her chest. "I must be married soon," he scolded himself. His desire was that of any healthy man in his late twenties. He could not wait to hold Novice in his arms and kiss her fully and properly as his wife. She must agree to set a date for the wedding. She just must.

An invaluable treasure in my possession, as well as my sisters', are the letters that survive between Harrison and Novice from the years 1909 until their marriage in June of 1912. All through nearly 3 years, the aching heart of Harrison Moore is poured out upon the page. Novice's letters in return are more subdued, full of her daily life and, especially, her concern for her mother Lizzie's deteriorating health. We can only guess that this had to do with the eye problem Lizzie experienced, no doubt accompanied by debilitating headaches. The subsequent loss of the eye shows how dire was her condition. Novice was vexed and terrified, beginning to suffer a profound battle with depression. She refers to her state as "the blues" and says in a 1911 letter, "I am so blue and cannot seem to want to do anything." In a letter from Harrison as early as 1910, he speaks of the bottle of medicine he gave her to "help her condition."

Whether because of her worry over Lizzie's illness or fear that the demands of marriage would consume her and cause her ties to her family to be lessened, Novice was truly a reluctant bride. Harrison had begun in 1910, asking her to be his wife early on and all the letters hence beg for her hand and for her to set a date. By 1912, the patient doctor had come to his end. In the letters, he fairly threatens to break off the relationship and his heart is all but broken. One can feel his anguish as he writes. They discuss the sinking of the Titanic in April of 1912 with Harrison referring to "even the yokels out in the sticks" knowing about it.

By the Spring of that year, the relationship was strained to breaking. Novice finally assented and a June wedding was planned. The couple wed in the wide, airy hallway, presided over by the Associate Reformed minister, after Novice descended the same staircase as Lizzie had done in 1889. She must have been a vision in the delicate white tulle with its trim of pearls and silver. The fact that the wedding was held on a Wednesday is curious yet it was customary in the South for Wednesday afternoons to be a sort of holiday, with businesses closed and Dr. Moore taking a respite from his duties. Indeed, all his life, Granddaddy played golf on Wednesday afternoons well into his seventies.

The new Dr. and Mrs. Harrison Moore left by train for a two week honeymoon in New York. When they returned, Dr. Moore accepted a position in Spartanburg as a physician which he hoped would be more interesting and lucrative than in the small town of Newberry. His bride bid her dear parents farewell and became his wife in the comparatively big city. But not for long.

Novice was instantly tearful and homesick for her family and the farm. She began to spend long days, even weeks, in her old home with her mother. She used her mother's ill health as the reason for her absence from her needful husband. Finally, it became clear that Novice would not be consoled unless she moved to Newberry, so Harrison reluctantly abandoned the hoped-for career in Spartanburg.

Back he went to practice in the countryside and minister to the people of Newberry County. He lived in the home of his in-laws until he could afford to buy a home for himself and Novice. But, over the years, he began to see that this would never be. Novice stepped into the role of mistress of the house as Lizzie became more infirm each year. She accompanied her to the doctors in Columbia at regular intervals and stood by to nurse her back to relative health after the removal of Lizzie's eye. When Novice gave birth to a son in 1913 and a daughter in 1920, still she turned deaf ears to Harrison's pleas for a home of their own. As her husband prospered and achieved a fine reputation in the community as a trusted doctor, he tempted her with more and finer homes, palatial mansions in the lovely old town. His wishes were ignored. With a determination buried in her soul, Novice held sway, devoted to her parents and to the home of her ancestry. The rift in the marriage was to turn into a scar that could not be healed.

As the years passed, the couple would strive to maintain their lives, individually and as a married couple, living in the home of the Browns. The household had grown over the years to include not only two Moore offspring, Wilson and Mary Elizabeth, but also the Brown's son Chalmers and his wife Anna. Cousins Kate and Jo had been part of the retinue until they found lives of their own as teachers in Columbia. Never marrying, they eventually shared a home with their contentious sister-in-law Daisy after the death of their brother Tommy Thompson.

The Brown clan saw years of prosperity and those of hardship when the Great Depression hit in 1929. My mother, Mary Elizabeth, was a child of nine when the bleak years began. She has told of her grandfather, Wilson Brown, receiving the phone call telling him the bank in Newberry had failed and his life savings had been lost. She would never forget the color draining from his face and the look in his eyes. But the Browns and Moores were far better off than most of their friends and neighbors. They had an abundance of land and crops that produced if they could but find a market for them. Their garden was large and productive, enough to feed them and to share with the sharecroppers who remained paid workers. There were chickens for meat and eggs, hogs to be slaughtered and their meat cured, and cows that gave milk. They shared their bounty liberally. Doctor Moore attended to his patients whether they could pay or not. He was often paid in eggs, hay, or any foodstuffs his clientele could scrape up.

A family story tells of the time, on Christmas Eve in the early 1930's, when Dr. Moore was in bed with the flu. The family was gathered downstairs when there came a knock at the front door. A man, a patient of Granddaddy's who had long owed money, begged to see him. Nannie told him the doctor was indisposed but the visitor vehemently insisted. Granddaddy appeared in his bathrobe and the patient produced a hundred dollar bill--payment for the multitude of visits Dr. Moore had made on behalf of the man's family. A hundred dollar bill in those dire times was something to behold, to be sure.

During those years of the depression, money and food were hard to come by for most. Crime rates rose as people, frantic to find even a meal, resorted to any means available. Mother told of a time when there were bands of Gypsies in wagons and on foot, roaming the countryside in the Carolinas. One hot afternoon, when the wooden doors to the verandah were thrown open to catch the breeze, a group of Gypsies appeared and entered the house. Mary Elizabeth, a small child, was frightened as they spread quickly through the rooms, picking up anything that looked of value. "They were everywhere, in a flash," Mama said. Her mother Novice and grandmother Lizzie froze at the sight, speechless. Just as the horde began to ascend the staircase to the floor above, a tall figure emerged from the downstairs bedroom. Wilson Brown, Pappy, strode calmly into the hallway with his heavy rifle, cocked and ready. What he said remains a mystery. But the mysterious intruders dropped their bounty and fled out the front door. Only then did the women of the house collapse in tears.

Mary Elizabeth knew there was hunger in the nation and in her county, but the depression barely touched her. She was the darling of the family and the beautiful, intelligent, devoted daughter Novice had hoped for. Her goodness was offset by the rebelliousness of Wilson, her older brother whom she adored. Sent to military school at a young age by parents powerless to control him, his willful nature would be an issue all his life. He seemed to be following in his uncle Chalmers' (Bubba) footsteps, and indeed, the two developed a camaraderie that lasted all their lives.

When her daughter graduated from Erskine College, which had formerly been the Due West Female Academy, the alma mater of her mother and grandmother, Novice was disappointed when Mary Elizabeth chose a career as a lab technician in Atlanta and then in Florida. Novice threw herself into caring for her widowed father and her ever-distant husband. The depression that had haunted her all her life never abated. Indeed, as she passed middle age, her "spells", as she called them, grew more frequent. Residents of Newberry, dear friends and acquaintances, would find her disappearing for weeks, even months at a time, shuttered away in the protective rooms of the family home in the country. Then she would appear as if nothing had been out if the ordinary, smiling and acting her energetic, talkative self.

In 1951, in his ninetieth year, Wilson Caldwell Brown rode his stately Palomino, Maxie Lee, over all the acreage of the estate he had loved for seventy years. He cherished the memories of his life here with his darling Lizzie and had lived to see his grandchildren and even his great-grandchildren playing under the sturdy Live Oaks and Pecan trees in the backyard. That night, he took to his bed and by morning he knew his time had come. Faithful to his God all his life, he had no fear of death. With his daughter Novice and granddaughter Mary Elizabeth and her husband Joe gathered around his bed, he opened his eyes wide and whispered, "Novice, I see something." He was most likely given a glimpse of his future home as he took his final breath. The brave, kind-hearted, strong and wise son of the Confederate Colonel was gone.

Before her father's death, Novice had sunk deeper into a state of despair and the old gentleman was powerless to help her. His letters to his granddaughter, Mary Elizabeth, in Atlanta speak of bringing her there to enter a sanitarium. Doctors, even her own husband, were unable to heal her. Then, when Pappy died in July of 1951, Novice seemed lost. She struggled on but passed from this life two years later in 1953. Did she die of a broken heart over the death of her father? Was there too great a chasm between herself and her husband for her to find solace? Or did the mental fragility from which she had suffered for so long finally take its toll? We can only guess.

She left two children to carry on the legacy of life in the old home of her lineage. Her son, Wilson, showed no interest, preferring to live his life with his wife and child in Spartanburg. Only daughter Mary Elizabeth would love and care for the old land and house. She had been well brought up to feel it was her responsibility and the gift of her heritage. She would accept this gift, even its burden, until her dying day.

Thomas Chalmers Brown (Bubba)
Around 1915

CHAPTER FIVE

Anna and Bubba

The house shone with light. Light that streamed in through the freshly-washed windows. Light that bounced off polished silver and shining crystal. The month was June in the unusually balmy summer of 1956. Weeks of dusting, mopping, freshening and primping the house resulted in everything emitting a sparkle and glow to my eleven-year-old eyes. We were spending half the season on the farm, as usual. I had not reached the age when I would begin to dread the mandatory yearly retreat to the small town, away from my friends and Atlanta preoccupations. In the big white house surrounded by the leafy, cool green of summer in the deep South, I loved all the hustle and bustle, everyone assigned a task. I helped with the making of tiny bags of tulle filled with butter mints and tied with silver ribbon. These were "favors" to be given to all the guests.

Delicious smells emanated from the kitchen across the back porch. Extra cooks had been hired to turn out old family recipes. Nothing store-bought would be allowed. There would be the light, fluffy biscuits hand beaten by Carrie, stuffed with piles of ham that had been cured in our ancient smokehouse. Built in the early 1800's, the structure contained not a nail, but stout timbers, tongue and grooved to lock together. With its shingled roof sheltering the meat from the elements, pork in all its forms had been hung from its timbers and slowly smoked with hickory chips until curing occurred.

Thin slices of succulent sweet ham would be carved and piled on each biscuit, then placed on a silver tray and transported to the heavily laden table. Bowls of ambrosia sat swimming in stewing fruit and the fresh, hand-grated coconut that cook Janie Mae had laboriously struggled with all morning. Little tea cakes, frosted in almond icing, bore a sugar bell to commemorate the day. Pound cake glazed with lemon was sliced and offered along with rich chocolate devil's food and pineapple upside down cakes. Finger sandwiches of every sort were placed on Nannie's hand-painted platters and graced the long sideboard. My favorite was the creamy chicken salad on homemade bread with mayonnaise.

"Laurie! Stop pickin' at those sandwiches! We need every one of 'em!" my mother chided. And even though I found them irresistible, I tried not to think about the fact that one of my favorite hens gave her all for this important meal. In truth, not just one bird had been chosen to be sacrificed, I noted, judging from the number of drumsticks in the heaping platters of fried chicken.

To watch a chicken meet her fate in the backyard was a horrifying thing for a child, but also an early lesson in survival of the fittest and creatures being sacrificed so that humans could eat. I watched many times as Carrie corralled the prey in a corner of the chicken pen, then grabbed it by the neck as it squawked and fluttered. At that point, an unconcerned Carrie would begin to twirl the poor thing by the neck in a circle around her knees. I had to look away. The squawking ended quickly with the neck hanging limp. Then mercilessly, she found a good chopping block and hacked off the head, beginning to pluck the feathers immediately after the murder. In less than ten minutes, the future main course was carved into pieces, dipped in flour and dropped into a skillet of sizzling grease. Sad, but a mouth-watering entree to be sure.

"I know it's hard to watch," Daddy said to me one day just before we sat down at the table. He loved chickens in an unusual way and had raised them as pets in the backyard of his Ohio home as a child. "But think of it this way. Chickens are born to 'give their all' for our food." He gave butchering a poetic twist, as he did so many things.

"They don't know any different," he continued.

"Do, too," Bunny chimed in.

"No they don't," Daddy countered. "Their brains aren't even the size of a pea. They can't think." I thought about that for a long time. I wondered if certain humans couldn't think, either. Maybe it would be kind of nice not to think. I seemed to be one who couldn't stop thinking, all the time, about everything.

In a departure from the usual filling meal at noon, we were given a few of the tea sandwiches leftover in the kitchen. "Save room for the big party," Mama sang out. She was frazzled but happy at how the preparations were going. She pronounced 'party' in her best southern drawl when she was happy--'pahhhty.'

The occasion was the twenty-fifth anniversary of the marriage of my uncle Chalmers Brown and his wife, Anna Footman Brown. A celebration had been planned for my grandmother's brother and the woman he had married late in life. After a ragged bachelorhood marked by failed attempts at various careers and a struggle with the bottle, he had finally married.

"Bubba", his nickname, had met the spinster Anna Footman and a relationship ensued that seemed to suit them both. At thirty six, Anna's prospects were slim. She held down a secretarial job in the tiny town of Union, South Carolina, a nondescript sort of dusty Southern community where nothing much happened and nobody seemed in a hurry to change that fact. Bubba found the twenty five mile drive from his parents' home the perfect get-a-way; he hotfooted it to Union on a regular basis to drink at out-of-the-way honkytonks in a rare county that winked at Prohibition and where speakeasies abounded.

The spoiled Chalmers, "Bubba" as he was called, was difficult to control but loved by his parents; his smoking and drinking were overlooked as long as he brought none of it home. For Chalmers' part, he considered Novice the favorite and resented, despite his efforts, her stellar scholarship and devotion to her family. He determined at an early age to venture far from the little town of Newberry in an effort to see the world and taste of its opportunities. He was surly and argumentative, his father, Wilson, at a loss as to how to discipline the young man. Lizzie, stronger in temperament than her husband, stepped in to set boundaries but to no avail. In the end, Chalmers proved a formidable foe for everyone, a disruptive presence in the family with a reputation around town as a gambler and roust-a-bout. In an effort to lend him direction, Wilson and Lizzie funded his failed attempts to earn his fortune in various risky schemes. Each new idea would be the one, he promised them, to keep his interest and use his talents.

No one knows quite how Mr. Brown met the rather reserved spinster. But, in the spring of 1931, after a brief courtship, Bubba came home to announce his marriage to Anna. His father Wiss, mother Lizzie and sister Novice were shocked but happy. Novice had by that time been married to Dr. Moore for many years and was the mother of two children; she most likely hoped for cousins for her young offspring.

Bubba and Anna promptly moved into the family home where they occupied the big, airy bedroom at the top of the stairs to the right, just off the balcony of the second story. The windows faced the fields to the north and east and allowed nightly breezes. A vast fireplace provided warmth in cold weather. This had been Bubba's room all his life and he simply added a wife among his collections of guns, World War 1 memorabilia and natty suits. Bubba served in the army in the Great War and had come home to seek his fortune in such far-flung places as Chicago all at the expense of his father's capital. When he failed up north, he returned home for a short while, then took off for Florida to make his windfall in the land boom of the twenties. Again, he lost his father's confidence and generous investment in his son's future. Dejected, he returned to the only place he could go, back to the family land to become the farmer he never wanted to be. The carousing increased. The boredom weighed on him, living in his childhood room in his parents' home with his well-respected father and a successful physician for a brother-in-law. Then he found Union.

Now in the house, and up until the late 1950's when the newlyweds finally moved to their own home across the road, there lived the Brown-Moore clan, eight in all: Wiss and Lizzie Brown, Harrison and Novice Brown Moore with their two children Wilson and Mary Elizabeth, and the new Mr. and Mrs. Bubba Brown. Assorted cats, twenty by general count, lived just outside the back porch and a gentle German shepherd rounded out the menagerie. Large families often lived together in these years before and after the hardscrabble thirties when scraping out a meal often took more than one provider. The family was fortunate indeed to have a spacious residence to shelter them.

Somehow, the arrangement worked. Anna continued to drive each day to her secretarial job, often spending nights in her former room in a boarding house in Union to avoid the arduous trip. Bubba oversaw the running of the farm. His kindly father Wiss, now in his sixties, planted and maintained a large garden, raised hogs, chickens and cows and rode out weekly to hunt deer, rabbit and squirrel for the family table. Dr. Moore practiced medicine in town, except on Wednesday afternoons when the office was closed and he played golf. Matriarch Lizzie was in charge of the kitchen, planning meals for the household and supervising the two cooks. Novice had the task of overseeing the housekeeping, maintaining the help who hand-washed and ironed all the clothes for the family and kept the house cleaned and dusted. Freshly pressed linens were changed weekly on all the beds. The group dined together, three meals a day, with the exception of Anna who took her lunch in Union. Novice primarily sewed and repaired the clothing, canned the fruits and vegetables of summer for the winter table and saw to the upbringing of her son and daughter.

Bubba, the unhappy farmer, had harbored a propensity for drink possibly all his adult life, though the habit would surely have been frowned upon by his tee-totaling family. Wiss and Lizzie never imbibed even a hint of liquor and Harrison and Novice followed suit. On rare occasions, Dr. Moore would prescribe a "hot toddy" for his father-in-law's aching joints. A teaspoonful of warmed whiskey was mixed with a little honey or sugar and slowly sipped by the fire as Pappy rocked in his reed rocking chair. Only one-----only a teaspoon.

But Bubba's drinking was known by everyone on the place save his relatives.

The sharecroppers, descendants of former slaves whose ancestors had never left, watched "Mista Chalmers" make his way to the field each morning after dawn and a robust breakfast. He dressed each day in a khaki brown shirt and trousers with the pant-legs tucked into sturdy boots. A pith helmet fought off the sun. He looked for all the world as if he were going to war. He ordered the laborers to work in a gruff voice, then took up the hoe to hack away at the earth for a short spell. Then it was time for his morning refreshment, carried in a jug; a little mid-morning respite from the sun. The bell was rung from the tower in the backyard precisely at noon, signaling the midday meal for all hands. Bubba trudged home to eat the fresh bounty he had helped produce, then took his usual nap upstairs in the spacious bedroom which was quiet while Anna was at work. After an hour or more, he walked again to the fields where plowing, hoeing and planting were in full swing, overseeing his laborers. Around three he took his customary afternoon snooze after a long swig from the jug, laying down in the soft dirt. The workers snickered at his snoring but said nothing.

Years later, after Bubba's passing, we learned of his leisurely days spent in a stupor. Wizened Jesse, the last remaining sharecropper who died in 2010, related tales of the field workers watching Bubba nipping from the bottle, walking in circles, mumbling to himself. "He don't do nothin' but cuss at us and hoe a little, then he fall down and go to nappin'. He wake up and lay in the dirt and be laughin' up at the sky. Then he stagger aroun' and fall down till time to go up to the house fo' supper." Jesse, the grandson of slaves, laughed at the memory, but we were astonished.

The thing I remember most about that summer celebration for Anna and Bubba was how the house gleamed. All the silver and crystal was laid out on the vast dining room table with its delicate lace tablecloth. And how the air smelled in the whole of the house! Gardenias by the arm full had been cut from the multitude of bushes in the front and back yards. They drank from every vase to be found hidden in cabinets and filled the rooms with a heavy perfume which wafted upstairs to all the bedrooms. Sure footed Elijah, a sharecropper's son of about twelve, was relegated the task of bringing down magnolias from the branches of the tall trees at the edge of the property. He descended carefully, cradling the creamy blossoms, bringing them to the kitchen to be added to the vases.

Placing a bowlful of the beauties on an upstairs table, I was reveling in the glorious smell when Anna called me, unexpectedly, into their room. Bubba, dressed in his finest, was descending the stairs as I made my way timidly to her door. She motioned me inside in a rare invitation. I entered with reticence, having only seen the room on the rare occasion when I ventured a peek in their absence. I loved the huge, elaborately carved bed with its enormous headboard and the way the sheer voile curtains blew over the wide-board floors in summer.

Now I walked toward Anna as she held out a stickpin, beckoning me to help her secure a huge corsage to the shoulder of her soft gray, crepe dress. I thought she looked lovely and she smelled of lavender soap and lily of the valley cologne. Her complexion had never seen the southern sun, and it was pale and flawless, glistening with the merest hint of perspiration under her heavy white powder. Her hair was still a soft brown with a few streaks of silver. She visited a beauty parlor in Union regularly to receive a 'permanent' of finger waves, a holdover from the thirties she had never abandoned. The waves were like little ripples on a pond, only they never moved.

"Laurie, help me with this, can you?" she drawled. She seemed nervous.

"I tried but I just can't seem to...... and Brown is all thumbs," she stammered. She always called her husband by his last name, another peculiarity. I managed to please her with the outcome of pinning the corsage and she hurried me out of the room before making her appearance down the staircase to the polite greeting of the houseful of guests.

The wonderful scent of gardenias and magnolias lingered for days after the gala. It seemed a magical summer, those weeks in 1956, when I was eleven, my sisters eight and five, and my brother just a tot. I watched Bubba come from the fields for the noon meal and return wearily at the end of day. He smelled of whiskey and cigarettes, sweating through his clothes, spitting a vile brown stream that emanated from his lungs before entering the house.

He always scared me a little and had nothing to say to me. Thank goodness he and Anna never had children, although he seemed to favor my cousin Barbara and her parents, Wilson and Mattie.

Bubba at last made his feeling for his family known after he and Anna built their own home just across from the imposing white house of his parents. He inherited the tranquil acreage that he had been able to view from his bedroom window, forty four acres of prime pasture, and land on the far side of the house as well. A few years after Nannie's death, he sold the land to a buyer unbeknownst to the family, devastating my mother who had long wanted the property. She wanted no land to leave the family, a fact well known to Bubba. After an emotional, raucous scene, Bubba canceled the sale to the stranger and agreed to sell to mother. But the deal had changed. Now, he raised his price considerably in an act so vengeful the wound it caused festered over all the years of his and Anna's lives. At his funeral in 1961, my mother shed not a tear.

Aunt Anna lived alone in the house across the road until her death. She remained at a distance from the family, keeping ties with Wilson, Mattie and Barbara in a sort of vindictive camaraderie. At night she could be seen through the front windows, walking dreamily from room to room, admiring the spaces, pausing to polish a vase or dust a lamp. Surely she must have loved the freedom from her hard-drinking husband and, at last, a home of her own.

THE WATTERS ERA

Mary Elizabeth Moore Watters, (Mama, "Nano"), around 1937
1920-2002

Lt. Joseph Skead Watters, (Daddy, "Pop") around 1942,
1916-2008

CHAPTER SIX

Mary Elizabeth and Joe

A Memory

"I married him 'cause I liked the way he kissed", Mama drawls as she sips her Scotch. We girls, her three daughters, roll our eyes and laugh.

"What a reason!" I say, incredulous. Sally shakes her head in disbelief.

"Well, I married her because she had a convertible and pretty legs!" quips Dad, giving Mama a wink.

"I can't believe y'all got married after only knowing each six months," I continue. "It's a wonder y'all weren't in shock when you finally had to live together. You barely knew each other!"

"It's what most people were doin' back then, fallin' in love and gettin' married before the men were shipped overseas," Mama says. "We got married and I went with him as far as I could, to San Francisco. We were tryin' to get pregnant all the way out there on the train."

Dad has a gleam in his eye tonight, not only from good Scotch, but for his "Liz", the wife who saw him off to war in the Pacific. Married fifty three years in the autumn of 1996, my parents and their daughters sit around the big table in the kitchen they added after retiring back to the old home place. The house looks updated and comfortable with new furnishings brought from Atlanta mixed with old antiques that have been in the house for generations. In the parlor, the elegant tall windows of hand-blown glass are softened now with silk draping and the wide boards of heart-pine have been carpeted for warmth as well as style. Persian rugs bring a rich glow to the rooms. The linoleum in the "sitting" room, all the rage in the forties, had given way to tightly-woven, cut-pile covering that itched young legs and had to be cleaned with a "carpet sweeper". Now the room sported a new, softer carpet.

"Well, I guess the train trip was lucky for you, because here I am," I quip.

"Yep, probably should have named you "Wendy" after Wendover, Utah, right Liz?" Dad jokes after pouring another Scotch-rocks. "Seems like that's when it probably happened."

I watch my parents and I am still incredulous that the Southern Belle fell for the Yankee from Ohio and married him so soon after their first blind date. But the romance of wartime and the swaying Florida palms had cast their spell on the young Liz and Joe.

They were beautiful and lusty and the chaste Mary Elizabeth would never have relations outside of marriage. War loomed all over the world and one never knew when a life would end on the battlefield and love's opportunity would be lost. Joe put a ring on the finger of his lovely belle and, full of hope for a future free of war, their story began.

·····················

Born into a household of solid, churchgoing Scots-Irish men and women, Mary Elizabeth Moore had been a surprise to her physician father and his sensitive wife. The couple had resigned themselves to being the parents of an only son when Novice found herself expecting a baby in the spring of 1920. Their little boy, Wilson, was seven and tried hard to please his doting mother and distant father. In truth, he felt closer to his grandfather Wiss and grandmother Lizzie.

When his mother gave birth to a daughter on a warm day in October of that year, he was downstairs listening to the sounds of her labor in the upstairs bedroom his parents shared. Then he was brought to his mother's bedside and shown the plump, rosy cheeked bundle wrapped in the pink blanket.

"Wilson, this is your sister. Isn't she a beauty?" asked his weary thirty-one year old mother. Wilson didn't respond. He stared at the baby through bespectacled eyes and scratched his head. He didn't know what to think of his new sibling. But at least he would have a playmate now. The farm in the countryside could often be lonely for a small boy in a household of adults.

The baby was christened Mary Elizabeth after her two grandmothers, Mary Ellen Harrison of Spartanburg and Elizabeth Chalmers of the household. She was instantly the darling of the family, adored, cooed over and passed around from mother to grandmother to grandfather Pappy, to the kitchen cooks and housekeeping help. The child grew more beautiful with each passing year and proved a happy little girl and an astute student.

"I never got a 'B' until I went to college, only As", she was fond of saying as an adult. She was also proud of the fact that she walked every day to the three room schoolhouse a mile and a half down the road. As Dr. Moore's daughter, she was the favorite of the teachers and quickly became one of the leading belles of the town.

Her years at home were filled with parties and visits to other families in town and in the countryside. There were piano lessons and church picnics and weekends spent with her best friend "Rookah', a nickname for Lalla Rook Johnstone, daughter of a prominent in-town family.

When it came time to harvest the acres of cotton grown on the land, Mary Elizabeth begged to help. Her mother sewed a big bonnet to keep the sun off her daughter's delicate skin. She stitched a little knapsack out of calico like the ones made of burlap that the sharecroppers carried across their shoulders and which would be filled with cotton. Mary Elizabeth worked side by side with the workers as they toiled in the heat of September gathering the fluffy white crop which was the backbone of their livelihood, for both the Negro families and the Brown-Moore clan. No doubt this folly was short-lived by the little girl and scoffed at by the thirsty workers to whom the chore was sustenance rather than a game.

When Mary Elizabeth turned sixteen, she was a senior in high school. That she would go on to college was never in doubt and she discussed becoming a doctor and practicing alongside her father. She was voted "Miss Newberry" at her high school and took all honors at graduation being named Valedictorian.

Four years of college followed at Erskine, formerly Due West Women's College, from which her mother and grandmother had graduated. She was a chemistry and physics major and excelled in her laboratory duties. To say that Mary Elizabeth never rebelled would be an understatement. She did what she was told and followed family protocol to the letter. But her will was rarely challenged.

She tells of a time when her mother and grandmother took her to Columbia to shop for clothes. She loved pretty clothes and had closets full, even during the Depression when her father was often paid for his services with chickens and vegetables rather than cash.

"We were at Tapps department store, and I spotted a coat with a fur collar. I was told I didn't need another coat," Mama related. Novice tried to pull the screaming child from the store only to have her accelerate her tirade. Mary Elizabeth dug in her heels. She would not be moved.

"I refused to leave that store without that coat," Mama said with pride.

"Oh, go on and get it for her," Grandmother Lizzie chided Novice. Once again, as usual, the child got her way.

Mary Elizabeth was not an easy child to say no to. She told of the only time her father and grandfather ever had a cross word between them was over the disciplining of her brother Wilson. Dr. Moore had punished the boy by spanking him and Pappy thought the treatment too harsh. It was most likely that the sweetheart of the family never suffered such a fate.

The young Miss Moore was growing into a rare beauty in a town of beauties. She was petite with a lovely figure and legs that tapered into well-turned ankles. Her hair was a soft brown curled at her shoulders. Her skin easily took on the glow of the sun when she spent time out of doors and her eyes were a clear, crystal blue fringed with long lashes. But the outstanding feature that set her apart from all the other girls were her magnificent cheekbones. Her delicate face reflected the chiseled beauty of her Scottish ancestry with its long, sculpted nose and fine-boned cheeks and chin.

"Mama, you were such a beautiful southern belle," we teased one late Indian Summer evening in 1971, just after mother and dad had retired from life in Atlanta. The house sported a new aura and a grandeur that belied its origins as an upcountry planter's home. Refurbishing the old house of mother's ancestry had been a labor of love and it had become a proud showplace.

We sat on the front porch sipping cocktails, Mama with her usual Scotch. It had been a summer marked by scorching days and nights spent tossing in damp sheets. The old home never knew air conditioning as was the case for most of the south when we were growing up. The annual respite to the condo in Sarasota provided some relief, but when Liz and Joe returned to the farm in September, the heat had not abated. Now it was October and there was no hint of the cool, crisp air usually offered by autumn in the Carolinas. Everywhere, farmers were suffering, their crops burning up in the fields, their livestock searching for even a dew drop upon the morning grass. Cattle and horses lay limp under oak trees up and down the blistering asphalt and dusty lanes.

Rocking in her wicker rocking chair, Mama steadily sipped her drink, Daddy keeping it refreshed. "Bunny, go get one a' the fans and bring it out here," she begged. We knew exactly which "fans" Mama was talking about. In church on Sundays in the South, the heat could be oppressive. Each pew in the sanctuary offered several fans to the faithful to be used for cooling and, no doubt, to keep them awake. They were made of thin cardboard glued to a wooden stick and each had a scene of a praying Jesus or his portrait looking handsome and heavenward.

Bunny dutifully fetched the fan. As Mama fanned herself she continued, "Oh, y'all don't have any idea about what a southern belle is unless you've grown up here ("heah"). Livin' in Atlanta is not the real thing, I mean bein' a belle and all. I'll tell you about a true belle. Margaret May Armstrong. Now there is a southern belle." Mama referred to a lovely lady who lived in town, some years her senior. Margaret May was still a delicate beauty, even in her late seventies. Her flawless white skin bore not a wrinkle. Her thick brunette hair was always worn in a tight chignon behind her long neck. Merely a hint of silver highlighted it. She had velvety dark eyes veiled by thick black lashes and always burnished her full lips with crimson lipstick. I could not take my eyes off her whenever we visited the Armstrongs.

Mama continued, "When Carlton asked Margaret May to marry him, she said 'no'. Then he kept askin' and she kept sayin' 'no'. He was just crazy about her (she pronounced it "huh"). Finally, she said yes to him but she set some contingencies. She said she didn't get up before noon and didn't cook. He said fine, he'd hire a cook and she could sleep as long as she wanted. And all their married life, fifty some years now, he had driven those Armstrong children to school every mornin' because Margaret May was sleepin'. And she's never cooked a meal in her life." Mama laughed while we all just stared. Unbelievable.

So Mama was the town's great beauty and the high school scholar and queen of the senior class. But she was a good girl, too. Her friend Rookah made up for both of them, Mama said. One night, a sixteen year old Rookah was to spend the night at Mama's home after a date. When Mama opened the door to her, Rookah fell into the hallway, moaning and wretching.

"Daddy! Come quick!" Mama called. "Rookah's sick!"

Granddaddy took one look at Rookah and made the pronouncement. "Rookah's not sick, Mary 'Lizbeth. Rookah's drunk." The two friends were inseparable yet Mama definitely towed the line while probably frowning at Rookah's lack of control.

The college years went by in a flurry. Mary Elizabeth was the belle of the ball in her home town, but her college disapproved of dancing and no such events were held in Due West. So she danced up a storm at the cotillions and parties back home. She learned the jitterbug and was light as a feather on her tiny feet. Summers were spent swimming in the lake at the country club, "frog-giggin" as Mary Elizabeth called it. Boys and girls caught frogs in the dark at water's edge, probably sneaking kisses under the stars. But the doctor's daughter remained pure and fell for no man. There were vacations to the mountains and beaches as well as to the Chicago World's Fair in 1933. One summer, Mary Elizabeth visited Myrtle Beach and came away with a sunburn she remembered her whole life. She was so burned that large blisters formed on her body and face. She suffered with fever and chills and was admitted to the hospital for several days. But that never deterred her from loving the sun and getting a tan each summer of her life.

Back at Erskine, males and females were separated not only in dormitories but in class as well. There was very little contact but for the occasional afternoon tea or a gathering for a book review and on Sunday at church services. The students stood apart separated by a field and a fence, laughing and waving at each other during the week.

"But we had our ways," Mama smiled slyly as she sat on the front porch sharing stories of her girlhood. "We had a system of communication we called "wicketing". A boy or girl "wrote" letters in the air until we made a word and then the word formed a sentence. I was great at it. Lots of the boys pursued me but we couldn't really 'date' or anything. I didn't break any of the rules." She stared out over the darkening landscape of the land she loved so much, remembering. Sipping her Scotch, fanning with her delicate hand, she must have had an idyllic life and never caused a moment's concern for her proud parents. She was angelic and obedient.

Except for smoking. All the rage, cigarettes in the 1920's were becoming accepted by society as an indulgence to be enjoyed by both men and women. At age fourteen, Mary Elizabeth tried her first cigarette behind the barn and was hooked. She hid her secret, undiscovered, outside, until her father confronted her.

"Well, you might as well smoke inside", he said in his dry, stolid way. So the virtuous Mary Elizabeth puffed away all through the years of college (although "on-the-sly" at the strict establishment), inhaling through her halcyon years as a single woman in Atlanta, through courtship, marriage, motherhood and grand-motherhood until she suffered a heart attack at age sixty-four and was ordered to quit the habit. Then she stealthily "rolled" her own, using oregano, until she conquered her addiction a year later.

The young Joseph Watters couldn't have cared less that she was a smoker even though he never acquired the vice himself. His mother Geraldine and father Stanley both enjoyed tobacco as did most of the generation of Americans living in the years before the war.

The last child of a tire industry manager and a housewife, Joe was born in September of 1916 in an upstairs bedroom of his parents' house in Shelby, Ohio. He joined older brother Albert and had shared his mother's belly with a twin sister. When a daughter was born first, the midwife presented Gerri with her baby, then took another look. "I think there's another one," said the attendant. Another push delivered a four pound boy.

The twins were nursed simultaneously by their mother and the girl, called Sally, flourished. In contrast to his sister, Joseph was a thin, thoughtful child all through childhood. He was quiet and studious, preferring to watch the ants building their dirt cities while sitting on the back stoop of his mid-western home. He raised chickens as pets, naming each of them. Neither athletic nor boisterous, he was the opposite of his older brother. His father seemed to favor the robust Al, so Joe clung close to his mother and sister.

"When my parents went out for the evening, Al was in charge as the babysitter and bullied us. He beat me up and made us go to bed while the sun was still shining. I hated him," Dad said unabashedly. Even as an octogenarian, Joe recalled the harsh treatment. There seemed to be no love lost between the two brothers, but a kind of measured friendship born of mutual respect dominated their remaining lives as adults.

When the Japanese bombed Pearl Harbor in December of 1941, twenty five year-old Joe was attending church in Buffalo, New York where he had taken a job in retail management after attaining a master's degree. "The minister made the announcement that the Japs had bombed us," he said. "I knew the service would get me, so I went down and enlisted the next day. I wanted the Army Air Corps. There wasn't an Air Force so to speak until later." Joe was immediately given the rank of Lieutenant after acing the aptitude test given to all enlistees. He was the first soldier to rise from his seat and turn in his test. "Wow," said the instructor. "looks like we have an English teacher here."

That December of 1941, Mary Elizabeth was working in Atlanta as a lab technician at what was then known as the "Grady's." The present day Grady Memorial Hospital was a large charity facility housing black and white patients in segregated buildings. The young, pretty lab tech with the beautiful legs boarded in a house strictly reserved for females on Fifteenth Street just off Peachtree. She was enjoying freedom in the big city and making friends with others in the medical field-- clinicians, nurses and doctors. She experienced her first serious crush on an intern, Dr. Tom Rambo, a dark-eyed practitioner who wooed her with flowers and nights on the town when he wasn't toiling in shifts at the hospital. But Tom failed to exhibit any lasting commitment and when an offer of a job in Gainesville, Florida came Mary Elizabeth's way, she took it and headed south in her maroon Ford convertible, a gift from her parents.

Alachua County Hospital was a busy center of both civilian and military life. A nearby Army Air Base housed and trained men who had been drafted or signed up in the first wave of patriotism following Pearl Harbor. Joseph Watters was among the young officers.

Joe had accomplished a stellar career in high school in Ohio, graduating as Salutatorian. He acted in school plays and had a literary bent. Growing into a sensitive, handsome man, Joe never fell in love in those early years but he spoke of a redhead named "Dottie" who peaked his interest in romance. He went on to Ohio Wesleyan University in the little town of Delaware, where he again excelled as a student and spent much of the time in the home of his favorite aunt, Golda Lorraine Roberts, his mother's sister. It was a friendship that would last all their lives. When he wasn't dining with his aunt, he joined in the merrymaking at his Sigma Chi fraternity.

After receiving an undergraduate degree, Joe chose to study retail marketing and management, receiving his master's degree in 1940 from the University of Pittsburg. He was interning at a department store in Buffalo, N.Y. on December seventh of nineteen forty one when the Japanese devastated the Naval Base at Pearl Harbor and America was propelled into war. He knew he would be drafted so he chose to join the Army Air Corp as a Lieutenant. He was sent to Gainesville, Florida in short order to train. Florida would change his life forever.

When "Liz" was introduced to the young lieutenant as his blind date, he was smitten. Her soft drawl and southern manners, her lovely legs and quick mind enchanted him. And when they shared a kiss that knocked them unexpectedly off their feet, he knew he had found the One. He quickly proposed.

Liz had to think about it. She loved her career and knew that marriage meant an end to it and any future aspirations of medical school. As a wife, she would be expected to keep a home for Joe and give birth to his children. Life away from Newberry had opened up a whole new world for the sheltered doctor's daughter and she was having the time of her life. Nevertheless, good men like Joe Watters didn't come along every day even for belles like Liz. And oh, that kiss.

The First Presbyterian Church in Gainesville was the venue chosen for the small, tasteful ceremony on September 18, 1943. The groomsmen, three in all, were shipping out one by one in a matter of weeks. Mattie Moore, the bride's pretty sister-in-law, was the only attendant. Dr. and Mrs. Moore attended their daughter's wedding as did Geraldine Watters of Ohio, the mother of the groom. The bride was resplendent in white slipper-satin, with a long veil and delicate headpiece. She carried a bouquet of white orchids. After a brief reception, the couple departed for a weekend honeymoon at The Inn on the beach in Ponte Vedra, Florida.

A lifelong love affair began, not only between the handsome newlyweds, but between Mr. and Mrs. Joseph Watters and the whole, sun-drenched state of Florida.

While Daddy was away serving in the South Pacific, Mama moved back to Newberry and her parents' home. She happily discovered she was expecting a baby but continued as long as she was able to work as a lab technician in the same hospital where her father was a respected physician. In January of 1945, Dr. Moore delivered his daughter of a tiny, squalling four pound baby girl.

"It's a nasty little girl," was my grandfather's pronouncement. I was frail, weighing exactly the same as my father did when he entered the world in 1916. I struggled to breathe, my lungs full of mucous, possibly not quite developed. My mother's smoking probably contributed to the condition, a fact not yet recognized in the forties.

One of Mama's surviving letters written to my father tells of an afternoon shortly after my birth. Mother slept lightly in the hospital room, my grandmother by her side. Granddaddy entered and, in a whisper, Nannie asked how I was doing. "I don't give her much of a chance," said my grandfather, shaking his head.

Mama heard the remark and sat up in her bed, frantic. Her parents tried to comfort her. No doubt, back home on the farm, Pappy was on his knees in his pleadings for my survival.

His prayers were answered and I was brought to the house of my heritage and placed in a bassinette in Mother's room upstairs. I nursed well and grew stronger. My mother surely longed to cradle her child as I cried upstairs, but there was a theory, adopted by my grandfather, that picking a baby up between feedings would result in a spoiled child. So, according to my cousin Barbara and confirmed by my mother, I was allowed to cry alone in my crib while the family paced the floor and watched the clock downstairs. If I was suddenly quiet, someone crept in to find my dear Pappy holding and rocking me in defiance of his son-in-law's rule. Somehow I persevered, but surely there was a lack of the all-important bonding between mother and child and a need for love that haunted me all my life.

In the South Pacific, the battle raged between the Japanese and American forces. Joe, now a Captain with his regiment on Okinawa, stood at the front of an intelligence meeting for bomber pilots. His job was to point to targets on a great map, projected sites to be bombarded by the airmen. At the back of the room, Joe saw a fellow soldier wildly waving a telegram, grinning from ear to ear. Joe cut the session short and raced to his friend. "It's a girl!" shouted Captain Watters. "Leaky", as the squadron had christened him, was a father. Joe was overjoyed. He and Liz had discussed what sex they wanted for their first born, and a daughter would be ideal, they thought.

It would be another eight months before the B-25 Bomber "Enola Gay" dropped the atomic bomb on Hiroshima and the Japanese surrendered. Then began the slow matriculation, taking sometimes up to six months, whereby the troops were processed from active duty, making their way across the Pacific to Hawaii to the mainland United States, then crossing the country to resume their respective lives. Liz took the train out to California to greet her husband and the two came immediately to Newberry so that my father could meet his small daughter.

Joe's tenure at active duty in the islands of the Pacific was rarely discussed. From small radios in rain soaked tents, the music of Tommy Dorsey and Frank Sinatra wafted over the occupied islands of the Pacific while men in military-tan khakis mapped out missions for bombers and ground forces fended off the enemy. Even as the lush, sodden jungles hid enemy eyes and the white sands of paradise became soaked with the blood of the fallen, the men thrilled to visits by Bob Hope and Frances Langford and listened to songs from home, choking back tears and memories.

All Joe Watters would discuss, the only thing we knew, was that Daddy had slept in a tent, that it rained a lot; and that he had pulled his olive-drab army blanket tightly around his body, even his head, so the cat-sized rats would run over him at night without biting. He never talked of the horrors of war and what he must have seen. Only a few miles away from the airbase on Okinawa, U.S. Marines were fighting a brutal daily battle to keep the Japanese from overrunning the island. Certainly Joe and his comrades heard the guns and saw the smoke of war.

We knew nothing of his squadron, finding out only after his death that his was one of the most highly decorated units of all the Pacific theater. The bombing sorties to targets directed to them by Captain Joe Watters and the intelligence team resulted in victory. Like most survivors of the brutality of war, my father probably chose to bury the past and never remember the nightmare.

A first job with Western Electric in Burlington, North Carolina was followed by an offer to become an assistant furniture buyer for the Davison-Paxson company, a chain of respected department stores. Joe jumped at the chance and the little family moved to the "star city of the South", Atlanta. My mother was expecting a second baby and would go again to Newberry to be delivered by her father and spend her postpartum in the care of her nurturing family. But, first, the Watters clan moved into their new home on Cardova Drive, a gift from Dr. and Mrs. Moore costing the sum of $10,000. Granddaddy paid cash.

In Newberry, Mary Josephine Watters arrived on March 28th, 1948, an Easter Sunday. When the proud parents discussed what to call the red-faced four pounder with the tuft of blond hair, I piped in "let's name her Bunny, 'cause of the Easter bunny." The nickname was adopted and I began a new life, learning to share toys and time and trying to be happy about having a sibling. Bunny cried, as Mama said, for five months with colic. Nursing her day and night was the only respite from her wailing. Then, by accident, Bunny found the satin border of a blanket in her crib and began to suck on it. The endless crying abated and peace was restored, both in Atlanta and during the frequent visits back to the countryside.

Just when I decided being the sister of a three year old was not so bad, here came another baby. Sally Moore Watters made her appearance on November 9th, 1951. She weighed a respectable six pounds and was a beauty from the moment she drew her first breath. Rosy-cheeked with a tiny, perfect mouth, Daddy called her his "little rosebud" and was clearly in love with the child named for his twin sister. Busy with two other children, Mama called on Daddy to "take over" Sally. He fed her, dressed her, bathed her, changed her diapers and generally played "mother" to the sweet baby who hardly ever cried. She quickly became "his baby" and the apple of his eye, a status that never changed all the years of his life.

He must have been frantic one afternoon in the summer of 1953 when Sally was almost three. The day was warm and we three girls played in the backyard, me with my small pots and pans, making mud pies. Bunny pretended to be a cowboy on the range who rode home to eat dinner with his family. Sally sat in my play "kitchen" and patted mud pies as I taught her. For some reason, she loved to eat dirt. She sampled the 'pies' as she patted. Along with her dirt diet, she discovered a nickel in the grass and popped it into her mouth, swallowing it with the dirt. As fate would have it, it was a Saturday and Daddy was home from work. I screamed and he came running, saw Sally choking, raced to his baby and stuck a long finger down her throat, withdrawing the coin. She screamed a bit, then went back to eating dirt.

Sally waited each night for Dad to arrive home from the office and the two were inseparable. Bunny waited to get home from school each day to retrieve her 'bah' as she called the now ragged blanket edged in sucked-on satin that she had never abandoned from her days in the crib in Newberry. Mama had cut the 'bah' in half to wash one side while Bunny clung to the other half. On her wedding day, Mama presented the 'bah' to Bunny wrapped in a bridal package, in case she wanted to carry it down the aisle!

On May 18th, 1954, a much welcomed son joined the Watters household. Stanley Harrison Watters was born in Atlanta, a blond, blue-eyed bundle named for his maternal and paternal grandfathers. He was surely a gift to the grieving Mary Elizabeth who had lost her revered mother Novice in

July of 1953. The fact that Stan (then called Sonny) was created even as Novice was being called to heaven was not lost on the couple.

Back in Atlanta during the school year, we had moved to a new neighborhood into a brick ranch-style house to accommodate our growing family. It was in a solid middle-class section of Atlanta with young families, most of which were headed by upwardly mobile young veterans returning to a booming America following the bitter world war. Mothers stayed home with their children; we played outside in backyards with clotheslines and thought nothing of riding our bicycles blocks down the street to play with other kids. Nobody watched us, no danger lurked on suburban streets. We came home at suppertime after being out in the woods and yards for hours.

Surely Liz and Joe must have experienced the highs and lows of any marriage. But their commitment was their bond. Joe, in love with his wife and proud of his family, possessed the easy-going nature needed by Liz. She was his queen, as she had been a princess growing up on the farm. Her desire to please her parents never waivered and her determination to nurture the home and heritage of her family was her driving force. Joe was a willing partner in making his wife happy and fulfilling her wishes.

When the retail industry grew more competitive in the late sixties, Joe found he was happier when he had been a furniture buyer, before the promotions and responsibility of management. The increased salary was nice, of course, and afforded a larger home in Atlanta in a fancier neighborhood, a country club membership and private schools for his children. But the pressure was great. He parted ways with his employer in 1970 and he and Liz made the decision to retire back to the old home place in Carolina. He was just fifty four years old.

After some soul searching and a period of possible mid-life crises, Joe returned to his childhood love of raising chickens and entered the industry full bore. He had two huge chicken houses constructed in the rear of the property and set about to become the gentleman farmer. He made friends in the little town of his wife's upbringing and joined in the social life of its citizens. The following years were good to Liz and Joe and they relaxed on the verandah as Mother's ancestors had done before her. They traveled often to exotic locales, falling in love with Italy and romantic Kenya with its safari life.

To Mama's great delight, grandchildren arrived to visit the farm and spend summers playing in the cool backyard of her youth. Liz and Joe were to live in the idyllic Carolina countryside until their deaths in 2002 and 2008 respectively.

Mary Elizabeth Moore had done well. She had been the obedient daughter who carried on in the manner for which she had been groomed. She had married a man who, out of love, had adopted her dreams as his own. The Sloan-Chalmers house built by her Great Grandfather had now sheltered six generations.

Her ancestors were smiling.

CHAPTER SEVEN

The Fifties

Summer rains in Newberry could last for days. We children were trapped inside, unable to run in the vast backyard. On sunny days, our general routine was to rise around eight, long after Granddaddy had left for his office. Mother had been up early to spend time with her mother in the early years and her father after Nannie's death. Breakfast was saved for us, usually eggs and bacon, ham, biscuits and grits. Our favorite treat was a specialty of Carrie's whereby she rolled the last of the biscuit dough into thin strips, dropping them into hot grease to be fried. They puffed up into airy pastry to be served with butter and jam. "Puffs" were a southern tradition not to be missed. After breakfast, we dressed and ended up in the yard to play until the big noon meal was served on the back porch table.

The backyard was a really a huge sandbox with patches of grass. It was flat and the soft, gray-white sand was perfect for bare feet. Chickens were released from their coop to roam freely, pecking at the corn scattered for them each morning by Carrie. We watched them eat, then chased them for a while. Usually, the chasing turned into a game of tag or hide and seek as we hide under the bushes and behind the various outbuildings around the yard. As the sun grew higher, my imagination kicked in. Bunny and Sally followed whatever adventure I concocted for us. I was the boss.

Massive pecan trees, planted before the Civil War by Thomas and Jane Allen Chalmers, stood at the back of the yard, their graceful limbs swooping toward the ground. One particular appendage took on a horse-like demeanor as it grew sideways, a few feet off the ground, and we climbed on it daily, commandeering our steed. I got on first, pulling Bunny up after me, then together, we hoisted little Sally behind us. With all our might, we pushed and bounced until the limb vibrated up and down, galloping across the plains of our imaginations. When I was tall enough to touch the ground with my toes, I gave us a shove and we sprang even higher, shrilling with laughter until one of us fell off or just got bored.

Next, we moved on to playing house. There was an adorable wooden structure at the side of the yard by the kitchen that had been Mother's playhouse as a child in the twenties. It had a door and real glass windows and shelves inside. We liked to play for a short while inside it, but preferred the sunny backyard. The soft sand was the perfect canvass for drawing out our imaginary house. With a broom handle, we mapped out the rooms-- a kitchen, living room and bedroom.

"You be the wife and I'll be the husband and I'll come home from work," Bunny said. "Sally can be the baby."

"Okay, but what if you're a soldier and you come home from a war?" I suggested.

"Yea!" Bunny loved the idea. "I'll go get my army suit on." At around age six, Bunny had been surprised at Christmas with a miniature khaki army outfit. Where Santa had managed to find it, we could never guess.

As she ran inside to find her khakis, I set about furnishing the rooms of our sand house with orange crates and cardboard boxes scrounged from the outbuildings and shed. I begged canned goods from Carrie for the kitchen and stacked up little pots and pans and tea set dishes. I ordered Sally to find acorns, rocks and leaves for our "soup" and she brought back handfuls of goodies for our table. Then she loved to sit, making sandy pies topped with leaves and nuts after I provided her with water from a spigot.

Thus we played outside in the sunshine, drinking in the fresh country air, running free like wild ponies as we dashed over the yards and hid under the branches of trees and bushes planted by our ancestors. We didn't realize it then, but, no doubt, William Chalmers had chased his sisters, Dollie, and Fannie who had hidden from him in the lush foliage even as their father Thomas prepared to leave for war in 1861.

But when it rained, I was cross and bored. In the fifties, a television had either not been purchased and, when one did stand in the family room, it was a novelty and offered only sporadic programming, usually at night. We sat for a long time watching a "test pattern" with the image of an Indian chief in full headdress, hoping some show would appear. When nothing happened, we sighed and wandered off to make our own adventure. I invented a scenario to entertain us on dreary days that we all remember as one of our favorite ways to spend the hours in the sticky rooms while sheets of rain poured down the window panes.

My muse was an old Victrola in the parlor that had to be cranked by hand. Nannie kept a collection of heavy, thick records from the jazz age in the huge cabinet beneath the turntable. Al Jolson belted out his classic "Mammy"; Eddie Cantor crooned and Nelson Eddy and Jeanette MacDonald trilled the duet "Look for the Silver Lining". Mesmerized, we were compelled to perform. A show was in order. We pulled the heavy coffee table into the middle of the room to act as our stage. Bunny donned her army uniform and I found big hats, old dresses and shawls for Sally and me. I was the diva, singing along as the soprano sang. I sank to my knees in order to be the same height as my handsome baritone, Bunny. Sally wanted to sing too.

"You can't sing," I said. "There's only two people on the record."

She started to cry. "Mama! They won't let me sing! I wanna be in the play too!" Before Mama came to her rescue, I found a butterscotch in a glass candy dish and bribed her.

"Take this as a treat. You be in charge of lighting. Very important job. Look. Let's bend the lampshade back on this big lamp. See? Now it's a spotlight. Roll it around and shine it on us when we sing." Sally felt important now, loving her new job.

We practiced for hours until we knew the words by heart and Sally morphed into a lighting expert equal to Broadway. Nelson Eddy (Bunny) lifted his deep voice to the ceiling in perfect pitch. Bunny had an uncanny ability to sound like a man. As he held Jeanette (me) in his arms, I looked wistfully into Nelson's eyes as Jeanette's quavering soprano filled the room. When we were ready, we called Nannie and Mama into the parlor and showed them to their seats. Announcing ourselves, Sally focused the spotlight on us and we cranked the Victrola. At first the speed was too fast and we sounded like scurrying mice. Then the tempo calmed and the beautiful melody transported all in the room to the Canadian Rockies with Jeanette and Nelson. The performance ended to applause and bows. As Sally took her bow, the pink porcelain lamp/spotlight came crashing to the floor. The pretense was shattered. Mama and Nannie were furious; we were in tears. But that didn't stop us. Every rainy day, we fired up the Victrola and put on more shows with costumes and roles for all. Except no lighting technician.

As the long, sweltering days of summer wore on, even we inventive children grew restless. We were taken to swim in the city pool and then the country club pool when Granddaddy became a member. I learned to swim swiftly and well in the long lanes of the town pool and was invited to join the County swim team. But we had to return to Atlanta and I couldn't accept.

Another foray we did to off-set our boredom, accompanied by mother and Nannie, was to go for a ride in Nannie's big Lincoln, out into the country, to see the sights. Down the two lane road we went, taking in the sights and sounds and smells summer. I remember being enchanted by the view of the magnificent old home in which Pappy had been born. It stood forlornly at the end of a long dirt road. I remember it seemed haunted, its white paint peeling to the bare wood. It appeared to lean slightly and Mother told us that it had been abandoned, somehow, by the Browns and left to go to "rack and ruin", as she called it. She said that vagrants had lived inside the beautiful old place, using the spindles from the staircase as firewood. Even at that tender age, I sensed the shame of this.

Down the road "apiece", as Southerners were likely to say, there sat Molly's Rock. Another haunting site, it was a huge rock off the main road, situated in a small pasture. The outcropping of rock boasted a large overhang providing protection and shade. It was very nearly a sort of cave. The tale was told of a "crazy lady", said Mama, who lost her husband and everything she owned in the Civil War. Her mind was one of the things she lost, so folks were reluctant to take her into their own homes. "They were afraid of her", Mama explained when we expressed our dismay at the lack of compassion. So Molly (I never knew her last name) lived under the rock all her life, scrounging for sustenance and grateful for the charity of a little food and water.

A thing my sisters and I both loved and hated was "visiting"-'visitin'—as it was pronounced. We made our way down country roads and into the shady streets of Newberry to call on various cousins and aunts. Uncles were usually not around. We children were left to our own devices while the adults chatted. We roamed the yards of the owners, played with dogs and cats who lazed in the sun, and generally killed time. We were always offered treats, usually cookies and little cakes, and the ever-present iced tea and sometimes freshly squeezed lemonade. Inside their houses, the 1930s held sway with furniture and architecture from those years the norm. Tall ceilings and board and batten siding inside fascinated me. Long hallways extending from the front porch to the back stoop, with all rooms exiting off this hall, seemed cavernous. I peeked in as often as I could.

A memorable visit one summer was to the in-town home of cousin Nina—(pronounced 'Niiine-ah'). Theirs was a stately mansion on a quiet street downtown with lovely verandahs up and down the levels of the house. Nina served her refreshments in the side garden of her yard, a magical place. I will always remember the huge blue and lavender hydrangeas that fairly leaned from the weight of their blossoms. Honeysuckle wrapped itself on the white fence in profusion and magnolia trees, their leaves so shiny they reflected the glint of afternoon sun, kept the yard cool and fragrant. Nina's rose garden shone with delicate pink tea roses and other blooms burst forth in a tangle of pale hues. I was enchanted. Our gracious hostess served fresh lemonade and cut slices of pound cake to be placed on thin china plates. She had brought her finest sterling spoons and forks into the out- of- doors, a fact over which my grandmother exclaimed. A table in the center of the garden was dressed in a linen and lace tablecloth. The pound cake was something I remember to this day. I have tried in vain to recreate its astounding taste and aroma. I savored the slightly almond sweetness as I bit into its airy texture and the sweeter-still lemony tang of the thin icing. Southern cooks were, and are, one of a kind.

When Nannie died, things weren't ever the same around the old house. Her love for us permeated every room imbuing all our antics with a feeling of excitement. Whatever we did, from the simplest of colorings on paper to a performance in the parlor, we knew she would praise us and think we were brilliant. It was as if a fresh breeze had been sucked out of the house, or a fine fragrance from some sweet blossom had drifted through the rooms until the flower wilted and was gone. When Granddaddy's sister Aunt Louise took the role of elderly caregiver to her widowed brother, her enthusiasm lacked something. We weren't her real grandchildren; they lived up-country near Spartanburg and I could tell she missed them. She was kind to us but Nannie's happiness at our visits, her all-engulfing warmth and nurture of her 'gran babies' could never be repeated.

But Granddaddy scared me; scared all of us. He was silent around us children, giving us the compulsory hug whenever we visited him in the old house in the summers and holidays, then, for the most part, ignoring us. By contrast, Nannie had been effusive with kisses, squeezing us to her large bosom, smothering us while she squealed in delight. Dr. Moore was straight and stiff, chewing his pipe between his teeth and speaking primarily to Mother and Daddy and, less often, to his wife. He talked mostly about medicine and various patients he had seen with interesting afflictions. He spoke about the farm and what it was producing in an off-handed manner. His life, it seemed, revolved around his tiny doctor's office in town just off the square across from the old courthouse.

We were taken there, terrified, each summer to receive our annual vaccinations against the feared childhood diseases of polio, tetanus, whooping cough and diphtheria. His soft-voiced nurse, Helen, gave us the injections and was tender and comforting. When she was on vacation, Granddaddy did the sticking into our tiny arms with the same stalwart demeanor he exhibited at home. No soothing words, just an admonition--"no cryin'".

I don't remember ever a gentle word from him, but one afternoon, I was dancing on the front porch after seeing an old Busby Berkley film on the small 1950's television in the den. I became, without question, not one of the dancers, but the star, of course, descending the stairs in my flowing gown with an enormous hat decorated in flowers and ribbon balanced on my beautiful, long locks. I sang and danced across the wooden boards of the porch, using the stone steps as my marble staircase. My back to the open front door, I gazed across the road to the fields beyond and envisioned my cheering audience. I took a bow and blew kisses. When my performance ended, I turned to find Granddaddy watching me. He snickered a bit, the closest thing I can recall to a laugh. Embarrassed, I said nothing, running away around the side of the house.

But years later, when the old house was being cleaned out, we came upon letters from an adoring Granddaddy to his soon to be intended and her answers to him in return. Here was an entirely different Harrison, a man of poetic ardor and candor. His warm words written to his beloved revealed a soft heart and jaunty spirit; certainly not the all-too-stiff, aloof man we knew him to be. What happened in the ensuing years after their marriage to change him?

It is a mystery at which one can only guess.

CHAPTER EIGHT

Coming of Age

Newberry Summertimes in the nineteen fifties could well have been the inspiration for a Norman Rockwell painting: a picturesque farm set in the countryside, a sprawling white family home filled with treasures from multiple generations, fields ripe with cotton, gardens bursting with strawberries, tomatoes, melons, corn and beans. Idyllic for a child on the cusp of the teen years, these were, none the less, a time of becoming self-aware and learning life lessons about love and hate, bitterness, jealousy and desire. I raced through the leafy backyard and across the plowed fields like a young colt just released from the barn. Tall for my age, skinny and tan, I was growing into puberty and embracing life with a headstrong exuberance that often irritated my mother. She didn't quite know what to think of me and found herself lacking the firm hand it would take to rein me in. She used her harsh tone with me daily and I knew she found me irksome and unfathomable.

The summer I was eleven, two things happened that signaled my awakening as a female. Hormones, a term I had yet to learn, were beginning to bubble in the blood and I was noticing, really seeing, for the first time that boys were different and liked me and I liked them back. My future avocation as a femme fatale was about to be born.

Kay and Larry Fields were the only children living on the country road near enough to be called playmates. Somehow we discovered each other the year the Fields rented the abandoned house less than a mile away. The rudimentary home was little more than a cabin with a living room whose gray boards had slats where light shone through. A piece of linoleum, the green and white from the forties that we had replaced in our own room with carpet, struggled to keep cold air out. There was no running water and heat for the Fields was provided by a single wood-burning stove. A tiny kitchen abutted this space. There were two bedrooms, each occupied by two double beds. There was no bathroom save for the outhouse and the prerequisite wash stand on the sagging back porch. Creaking wooden steps led to the sandy back yard where, we learned, the Fields took turns every Saturday bathing in a large galvanized tub filled with water from a well. The whole of the house appeared to be one wind storm away from collapsing with its rusting tin roof and torn screened doors. My sisters and I didn't care. We were enchanted.

Kay and Larry banged on our door most mornings when they became aware of the station wagon parked in the yard signaling that the Atlanta girls were visiting. We cooked up adventures, always outside, involving everything from Hide and Seek to Cowboys and Indians. That blazing summer of nineteen fifty six, not a single leaf stirred for days. The heat built steadily through the day and culminated each afternoon in ferocious thunderstorms that dumped rain but failed to cool the blistering air. The dog days of summer were upon us and we kept the garden hose nearby for frequent drinks. On a particularly hot day as the five of us cooked up a scenario, I found wayward chicken feathers strewn on the ground and tied them in my hair. Kay and I became two Indian princesses of a fierce tribe defending their land. We used sticks fashioned into bows and arrows and pretended to have knives to fight our enemy, the cowboys. Larry was sheriff and his deputies were my sisters. The Indian war waged on through a truce called for the noonday meal and breaks spent sneaking into the garden to steal strawberries. We sweated and rolled in the dirt of the backyard, smearing mud for war paint. Larry was relentless, pursuing us with his deputies into the furrowed fields of cotton and shooting at us with his cap gun into the pine woods. My sisters did the same until Sally got bored and went inside to play dolls.

Then, we were cornered. Although Kay and I fought to kill all the cowboys, they managed to, or we let them, defeat us. Roughly, Larry caught my arm and pushed me up against the young oak tree near the back porch. He tied my arms behind me with the jump rope, warning me, "you stay there, squaw, while I look for that other injun'". His "country-boy" accent resonated. I stayed tied. Soon, Bunny and Larry came back with Kay as prisoner and tied her to another tree. Larry loomed close to me and for the first time I noticed how tall he was. He had bright red hair and wore a shirt with a collar and buttons that his mother had probably sewn. He smelled of sweat and pomade and freckles peppered his arms and face. Then I noticed those arms. They looked strong, wiry with young muscle. He pressed up against my shoulder and growled into my hair, "You ain't gittin' away now, you hear me, squaw? I don't care ifn' you are the chief's daughter. You my prisoner now and I'm a-taking' you to the jail. You and your friend here." Hop-a-long Cassidy could have taken lessons. Something rose in me as he drawled the words so close to me. I sensed that he liked being near me. He seemed to be inhaling my scent as I did his. I felt small. He felt powerful. I liked that.

The rest of the summer, I had what I now know was a tiny crush on Larry and I took every opportunity to be near him, knowing I was having an effect. I could tell he liked me, but he was twelve and his mama had possibly warned him about girls turning his head when he was so young.

Nineteen fifty six wore on and we spent the last weeks of the summer getting ready to return to Atlanta for school. On the last Sunday before we were to make the trip home, I could hear my mother calling me to come for supper but I couldn't move. I was glued to the television in the living room. Ed Sullivan was on and there was a singer belting out his hit song. He had a beautiful profile and his thick black hair was worn piled up on his head like the boys we called "hoods". These were not boys I should be interested in, mama told me. But I couldn't take my eyes away from the young man from Memphis who played his guitar and shook all over and wiggled his hips. The same tingly feeling I had gotten from Larry that summer was creeping its way over my skin and I felt at once drawn to the new phenom with the strange name of Elvis. Gosh. All I could think of was ---"gosh". Something was going on inside me. I didn't know what, but when I started school in the fall, I paid more attention to my hair and clothes and the way boys were starting to stare at me.

By the advent of the late fifties, summers still found us on the farm for weeks at a time. We played our games as usual but days at the country club pool were a welcome change. I was growing up, growing weary of Cowboys and Indians. Kay and Larry had moved on, their father finding work in another small town. Now their old rented house looked sad and appeared to sag even more without the happy family to tidy it and try to make a life there.

The country club had been on the outskirts of town for years but the pool was a fairly new addition. My grandfather had been a founding member. He was the town's favorite doctor and everyone knew my mother and accepted us, her offspring. So I was able to make fast friends as I encountered other teenagers in the cool, aqua water. Newberry girls took to me, asking me questions about Atlanta and the boys there and whether I had tried smoking or beer. The answer was no to both, but I certainly could expound on the topic of boys. They seemed to be all I existed for. By ninth grade I had broken many a heart but had yet to have mine left in pieces—an event not long in the coming. The girls in the small town were no different, spending sleep-overs talking incessantly about the males who attended school with them, dreaming of the muscles on the high school football players whom they only hoped would notice them. Life on the streets of the tiny town was kind, with the proximity of the drugstore or movie theater within walking distance from most of their homes. And so we wandered the sidewalks pretending to be on an errand for a mother or shopping when in reality we used eagle eyes to find the opposite sex. When a hot Chevy roared past and honked, the girls knew the guys inside and waved. We sat coyly at the drugstore soda fountain and ordered cherry cokes while waiting for a blue-jeaned lothario to amble through the door. Then we spent a quarter to see the latest film and barely saw the movie as we watched to see what boy would sit where.

There was something called a "canteen" that the ladies of the social society had requisitioned to be used as a place where the teenagers of the town could gather. It was nothing more than an old army barrack with a corrugated roof but it had a coke machine and a counter to buy hot dogs and, most of all, a jukebox. Weekend nights, kids gathered there to dance to Chubby Checker, Elvis and the Everly Brothers. Rock and Roll, despite its tenuous beginnings being harangued by southern ministers as devil music, had taken a firm hold and we be-bopped to the tempo while flirting with boys who approached us for a dance.

I had just learned the Twist in Atlanta and delighted in teaching my girlfriends how to execute the steps. The boys stood back in awe, but one guy stepped forward for me to teach him too. He took to the music and danced expertly from the start. I was instantly drawn to him and tried to calm down when he asked to buy me a coke.

"You like peanuts in yo' coke?" he asked with a heavy drawl. "I do. I'll putcha' some in." He poured peanuts in my coke asking, "You that girl from Atlanta, aren't cha'?"

"Yea, Dr. Moore's granddaughter. Who are you? You sure can twist."

"I'm Corey Jones. Don't know 'bout twistin' though. I don't have a lotta time for dancin'. I work mosta the time and I gotta practice football. I just picked it up from watchin' you."

Corey Jones was a year or two older than I was. He was not as tall as some of the other boys there, but I came to his chin as I learned when we slow-danced the first time. He was powerfully built and broad-shouldered and his arm held me tighter than anyone I'd ever danced with. He had an air of assurance that most high-schoolers lacked. He smelled of sawdust and fresh- ironed cotton shirt and wore his curly hair short in what was nearly a crew cut. There was something entirely masculine about him and I felt fragile, as if he could break me in two with one strong hand. I was smitten.

A bunch of us piled into his refurbished car, his pride and joy. It was old but painstakingly restored with paint waxed to a mirror shine and immaculate blue and white seats. I wedged myself next to him to make room for the others and we were off to see what was happening around town. Corey drove expertly, not fast like a kid trying to show off. I watched the muscles in his legs tighten under his chinos when he applied the brakes. There was something a little frightening about this boy, something like an animal about to spring, always at the ready, looking for prey. But I was not afraid, only fascinated. He wheeled into a gravel parking lot in front of what was easily a place off-limits to teenagers. The whitewashed concrete building was a honky-tonk and rock and roll blasted from its single door and window. I could see neon beer signs inside and people on bar stools through the wide doorway. Dancers writhed on the dance floor and every now and then the music shifted to a low, bluesy melody. Then more dancers crowded into the hot, pulsing throng and I watched in a kind of trance. This was certainly no place for kids our age. None in our group made a move to go inside as if we all were content just to watch the goings on from the safety of Corey's car.

Suddenly, someone in the back seat, a boy I didn't know, whispered, "Hey Benji, go on 'round back and see if ol' Dinkins is settin' back there. Ask him to go get us some beer. I got five dollahs—that oughta' work." He handed the money to Benji who got out and headed for the back of the building. Sure enough, in a few minutes, he came back carrying a paper sack with several bottles of a cheap brew. The beer was passed around with everyone swigging gulps. When the bottle came to me, I pretended to sip but actually drank nothing. I didn't like the taste and I knew drinking beer at fourteen, even in a safe little country town, was not something I should do.

Letting Corey Jones steal a kiss was something else again. When he dropped the others off at their homes, Corey made sure my girlfriend Lily and I were the last to be deposited safely at her house. I was spending the night with her so there was no need to drive me the distance out into the country to my grandfather's house. And for some inexplicable reason, I was glad of that. Glad not to be so totally alone with Corey Jones out on the dark, silent roads. Lily jumped out of the car leaving me to say goodnight to Corey. He wrote down my phone number and asked if he could take me to the movie the next night.

"Well, I'll have to ask my mama but it'll probably be okay. Just call me and I'll let you know." With that, Corey hugged me and planted a peck on my lips in a polite kiss goodnight. He pulled away from the curb and I walked at top speed into Lily's house to find her peeking through a window. We jumped up and down and squealed so loud we woke her sleeping parents. Then we got into our pajamas and giggled, plotted and planned until the wee hours.

Right before I fell asleep with the glow of a serious crush beginning to blossom, Lily said, hesitating, "You know Corey's a mill boy."

"A mill boy? What does that mean? All I know is, he's a hunk and I like him a lot."

"Well, it means I don't think he's the kind for you, is all. His daddy works in the mill. His mama sews for other people. He works at the mill part time too. He lives in one of those shot-gun houses over in Milltown."

"What's a shot-gun house and what's Milltown?" I queried.

"It's over there where all the mill workers live, right by the railroad tracks. We don't really hang around with them, our crowd anyway. A shot-gun house is a little teeny house where all the rooms go straight back. Like you could shoot a shot-gun clear through it from front to back. I'll drive ya' by there tomorrow and you can see. But I don't think your mama's gonna like you going out with somebody from over there."

I fell asleep confused. All the kids seemed to like Corey, but here was Lily telling me to keep my distance, in so many words. I wasn't allowed to date at fourteen back in Atlanta, but things in Newberry were different. My mother knew almost all the parents of the teenagers I was spending time with, and the town was so safe with each family watching out for the others' kids. It was a more innocent time in a simpler place. A good place to "cut your teeth on." What lay ahead for me in Atlanta loomed in the distance.

When I returned the next day, I bounded up the stairs to find Mama. I told her all about the canteen and meeting Corey. I left out the part about the honky tonk and the beer. "He wants me to go to the movies, Mama. Can I go? He's real nice and he plays football and works part time at the mill."

Mama paused. "The mill?"

"Yes, his daddy works there and got him the job. He's real nice....like I said."

I knew my mama and knew too when she was disapproving of something. I saw the look, heard the tone. "You said his father works in the mill too?" she asked.

"Yea, I think he does." I tried to act nonchalant but I knew what was coming.

"Well, I don't think that's really someone you should go out on a date with. He may be very nice but I don't actually know anyone who lives down there......I assume he lives in Milltown."

I begged and pleaded and pouted and when Corey called that afternoon I had secured Mama's permission against her will.

Corey took me to see a military drama about Korea; then he drove me to a park where we walked as the summer sky paled and lightening bugs came out by the hundreds. The night air took on the magnolia-laced scent of the town, its heady fragrance lulling me into a romantic fantasy of boy meets girl and love ensues. I was Audrey Hepburn falling hard for Carey Grant. But this was not Carey, it was Corey, the mill worker's son. He of the muscled arms and animal magnetism. Corey kissed me tentatively and acted the gentleman. Then, driving me home, he ventured, "I don't think your mama likes me so much."

I acted shocked and started to protest, but he stopped me. "You come from a different place, see. It may not be this way in Atlanta, but here we know our place. We'll just be friends, okay? I'll see you around, Laurie, but I can't fall for anyone like...." he paused. "You just too classy for me, is all. You gonna need somebody with lots more money than I'll ever have. Trust me. I know these things." He walked me to the front door, placed one more reticent kiss on my questioning lips, and was gone.

I told Lily all about it the next day and she seemed relieved. "That's what I was trying to tell ya' last night. There's a difference here. You just sorta' stay with your own kind." She put another 45 on the turntable in her bedroom and resumed practicing the twist. "Do you turn your feet too or just twist at the waist?" she asked.

I tried to pretend I wasn't hurt by the knowledge that I wouldn't be seeing Corey Jones again, at least not one on one. I was growing up and learning there were lines you didn't cross even when your heart was leading you.

Someone of whom mother did approve entered my life that summer, and he was fun to be with but not in the exciting way Corey was. Carter Rossington "ran with the pack", as my mother called the knot of friends I had made and with whom I spent most every day. Carter's father owned the mill and many others in the Carolina upstate and was a well-known mogul of the textile industry. Carter's mother was a little older than mine but they knew each other from the country club and were guests at the same parties. Her son was the scion of a family dynasty, the third child and only male, heir to his father's vast fortune and the presumed next mill owner himself. But Carter had other plans.

We, the "gang", sat around in Carter's living room one stifling August afternoon listening to the crack of thunder approaching from the south. His was one of the most opulent houses I had ever seen, either in the little town or back in Atlanta. A Greek revival masterpiece built in the late twenties, it had an air of elegance and pristine purity, as if no one could possibly live amid the gilt chairs and delicate tables perched on the aged Aubusson rug with its pale hues of yellow and rose. Rich oil paintings hung majestically on each wall and the room in which we sat was presided over by a large portrait of Carter's grandmother hanging over an intricately carved mantle. There were fresh flowers everywhere, cut, Carter said, from the garden his mother cherished.

As the sky darkened, we lazed on the yellow silk brocade sofas and chairs. Charlie tinkled at the grand piano and we flirted and teased each other, all trying to be more clever and witty than the next. An affable black servant brought pound cake and lemonade and Carter regaled her, sending her into fits of laughter. I could tell she doted on him and probably had been a part of their family for all of Carter's life.

Records spun on the player and we sang to Elvis and Buddy Holly. We talked of the plane crash that had killed him and wondered what songs he would have given the world had he lived. The natural tension between the sexes rose and fell as the afternoon wore on. Lily and Benji were deep "in like", as she called it, stopping just short of being in love. They kissed as they sat among the deep Eiderdown pillows, Lily leaning her head on his shoulder. Carter kept staring at me. I could tell he thought I was pretty, but he wasn't my type. Small boned and thin, he liked poetry and wanted to be a writer. He wanted nothing to do with his father's mills, he said, and vowed to leave Newberry as soon as he could decide on a college.

"I want to live by the ocean and write, maybe have a pretty big boat. I'll date a girl and never tell her my last name. In fact, I'll make up a name and she won't know my real one until we are so in love and engaged. Maybe I'll tell her then. Or maybe I'll get married and then tell her. I want somebody who thinks I'm just a poor writer barely scraping by. Knows nothing about my family or this house or anything," he pontificated.

"Lotsa luck," Benji piped up, stretching his arm and nuzzling Lily's neck. "Can you get Ettie to bring more pound cake? Law' that lady can cook!" He used the southern word 'law' when others would have said 'Lord'. No taking His name in vain. And instead of "I swear," proper southern ladies and gentleman always said "I swanee" or "I swan".

Deena, the cheerleader who I knew didn't like me very much, said it as if on cue. "Well, I swan, Carter. Here's a Nina Simone record.....that one my mama won't let me listen to. The words are 'sposed to be pretty racy, they say. Let's play it!"

Carter quit eyeing me long enough to pop the record onto the player.

When he came back to the group, he squeezed in beside me. His hand found mine as we listened to words that shocked our virgin ears.

"Forbidden Fruit" was its title and Nina Simone, in her sultry, throaty voice, crooned "Go on and eat, forbidden fruit; it's mighty sweet, forbidden fruit; it's quite a treat, forbidden fruit; go ahead and taste it, you don't wanna waste it; go ahead and bite it, I bet you'll be delighted". We squealed with abject horror at the risque' words. None of us had heard anything like the lyrics contained in this song. As Nina sang of temptation and its delights, I felt embarrassed as Carter's eyes bored into me. I took my hand away from his in an effort not to encourage him. He was cute, had a great personality and brains to boot. Someone my mother would like immediately. But the electricity I felt with Corey was missing. When Carter asked me to go to the country club dance with him the following night, I readily agreed, wanting to please Mama and show her I knew what kind of boy I should be dating.

The country club in the little town was where society gathered for golf, dining, parties, and swimming in both its pool and lake. My mother swam in the lake when she was a girl and went on "frog gigging" expeditions. She had confessed that this strange pastime was an excuse for boys and girls to be alone and perhaps hold hands or steal a kiss. Now, thirty years later, little had changed. Carter whirled me around the dance floor until I was dizzy. He brought me punch and a piece of coconut cake, then asked if I'd like to take a walk around the lake. I thought about mama and the frog gigging, but decided I could handle Carter. I managed to keep him at bay until we said goodbye to the others and he drove me home. We had enjoyed the dance, laughed a lot, but he kept staring at me the whole night, telling me how pretty I was. I brushed it off as an empty compliment. He was just a friend, no one I could ever fall for.

When he pulled up in front of our house, he turned to me as if to try for a kiss. Although I was taught to let the boy open the door for me, I didn't wait. I jumped out of the car and began walking up to the steps that led to the front door. He was right on my heels. As I reached for the door knob, he reached for me, planting a lalapaloozah of a kiss on my glossed- pink lips. This was no ordinary kiss. With the experience of a matinee idol, he parted my lips with his tongue, bending me back and pressing against me. I jumped back in surprise.

"What's wrong? Haven't you ever been French kissed, big city girl?" he teased.

"Well.....uh......no." I stammered. He laughed a little, squeezed my hand and was gone. I stood there for a while, after he drove away, contemplating what just happened. I had been kissed on the same porch, in the same spot, as my mother before me—kissed where my grandmother and her mother had been kissed. I hoped it had been better for them.

I was in a daze as I brushed my teeth and got into my nightgown. So that was what all the buzz was about. I had heard about French kissing, but it sounded disgusting and there was no one I'd met who I wished would try it on me. Certainly not Carter Rossington. I fell asleep in a bed on the sleeping porch listening to crickets and the sounds of the farm settling in for the night, wishing that kiss had been shared with a boy from the wrong side of the tracks.

So, that summer of nineteen fifty nine, Buddy Holly was dead and Elvis was in the army. In a short while, James Meredith, brave and black, would seek an education alongside white students. And a little country in South East Asia called Vietnam would shape my generation and cause us innocent babies of World War Two to question our parents' belief system. The war that raged there would claim the life of Corey Jones. I was no longer a French- kiss neophyte. I had fallen for the type of man I would fall for the rest of my life and attracted the type I always would attract, but couldn't love.

Love, especially the getting of it, was the focus of my life in those teenage years of uncertainty. Beauty was all I seemed blessed with and I thought it was my ticket to a happy life. Women in those years, especially in the South, were expected to marry and raise children and rarely sought out a career. I thought little of earning my own way, intent on finding a worthy husband. I'm sure I expected to lead the kind of life my mother had done, as the wife of a executive in some field, living in a beautiful home with household help and socializing with prominent acquaintances. In college, I met a few girls with different ideas about their futures, but the majority of us wished only for the pampered life of a well-married matron.

Things began to change after the war in Vietnam. Women found their voices and sought to use the education they had worked for or been given. No longer was staying home and striving for perfectly light-reflecting kitchen floors enough. This was a huge conflict for me and I sought answers. The one place I found solace was back on the farm in Carolina. I took my children to play often in the backyard where I had so many fond memories, and shared evenings with my family on the wide verandah where Thomas and Jane Chalmers had watched the setting sun a century before. A peace I found elusive in Atlanta was to be found in the quiet countryside of my ancestry. Finally that search led me, in the Spring of 1970, to -- as Thomas Chalmers knew--the True Rock. The love I sought was to be found at the foot of a Cross.

But that coming of age summer, as I awoke in the ancient rooms where Lizzie and Dollie and Novice and Mary Elizabeth had risen each morning, I listened to the gentle wind and watched the delicate linen curtains blow in the cool of a country dawn. I dreamed of falling in love and heeded my mother's voice.

I learned there were classes of those who were acceptable and those who were not. And I learned to question whether I agreed with any of it.

CHAPTER NINE

Christmas Gift!

The phone rings every Christmas morning no matter where I am. "Christmas Gift!" says my brother Stan calling from his home in Washington, D.C. Then, later on, 'Christmas Gift!" cry Sally and Bunny as they phone from Richmond or Charleston.

The first person in my family of fourteen who has risen to make the coffee on Christmas morning as we gather in Jacksonville or Atlanta or Charleston or Vero Beach has the pleasure of wishing all the other sleepy revelers "Christmas Gift!" as we tumble out of bed. It's tradition now. Has been for as long as any of us can remember.

Christmases in Newberry, from a time long before I was born, can only be described in one word…..Glorious. The term "Christmas Gift" began when, after the Civil War, sharecroppers on the Chalmers' farm came to the back yard on Christmas expecting the promised seasonal remembrance from the Chalmers, then the Browns, continuing into the twenties with the Moores, in the forties and onward with the Watters'. The Gift usually consisted of a monetary bonus along with baskets of fruit and sweets for each family living on the property and working the land. At the end, only faithful Jesse Johnson and his wife Catherine were left in residence when Liz and Joe retired to the farm.

So our ever-expanding clan took up the call amongst ourselves. Now, tradition has evolved to mean that the first person to shout out the greeting must be given a gift by the ones receiving the request.

Christmas morning in the years of the early beginnings of the house would have found Thomas and Jane Chalmers surrounded by their menagerie of five children and various cousins, aunts and uncles and grandparents. In the lean years of the horrific war, it would have been a bittersweet gathering as Thomas would either have been absent from the family or had been given a brief respite from the fighting to travel the distance from Charleston to Newberry for a short visit. Later years would have found them happier and cherishing each year of peace after the terrific conflict that tore the nation apart.

With daughter Lizzie's marriage into the prosperous Brown family, times improved and she was possibly the matriarch who began the tradition of sumptuously decorating her family home with husband Wilson's blessing and amusement. A Christmas tree was cut from the pasture, probably a tall cedar, and adorned with delicate Victorian ornaments, many imported from Europe. Glowing candles graced every surface as fireplaces crackled in the tall-ceiled rooms. Dinner would have been a feast prepared by extra cooks hired for the occasion—turkey, ham, fresh vegetables from the garden, sweet potato pie topped with melted marshmallows, rice and gravy, several pies for dessert and the traditional ambrosia with its hand-peeled fruit and coconut grated in the kitchen by the elderly aunt Rose. The smells emanating from Lizzie's kitchen must have been heavenly.

Her daughter Novice carried on in like manner. These were the years when I came along and was the happy recipient of all the magic. Nannie went 'all out' in creating an atmosphere of love and bounty, even hiring a florist to adorn the rooms with all manner of seasonal blooms and glittery finery. The pile of gifts under the tree, still a cedar cut from the pasture, grew to overflowing. Dr. Harrison Moore, beloved by his patients, took all afternoon to open the plethora of ties, boxes of sweets and nuts, pipe tobacco and handkerchiefs bestowed on him by his loyal clientele.

Bunny and I raced down the stairs on the cold morning singing "Jingle

Bells" as mother had instructed. Then Sally joined us in the early fifties. Sally and I received frilly clothes for our new dolls and tiny tea sets. Bunny asked for, and got, Cowboy outfits and Army suits. Stan came along in 1954 and added to the melee of squeals in the parlor.

There was something about the very air, a smell of December chill and crispness that permeated my senses. Inside, the house was heated only by long-standing fireplaces and wood and gas stoves added over the years. I ran from room to room searching for warmth, my cheeks prickly with the cold until the fire warmed my skin. The cold hallway in the center of the house was quiet and sounds from each room, conversation and laughter, was muffled. Outside, the crunch of Oak leaves underfoot said, "it is Christmas Day in the South and all is right with the world." No cars passed by; the quiet was broken only by the lowing of a distant cow or the faint squawk of geese on a pond in a far field. The peace of it is in my soul forever.

When grandchildren were born to Liz and Joe, Mother continued the traditions set forth from the mid-1800s. The beautiful house was even more inviting as she added Christmas branches and shining balls and glitter to each room. She began the cooking for the traditional meal weeks ahead and was often visibly worn out by its end on Christmas Eve. She had found it better to celebrate the great feast on Christmas Eve, but added a sumptuous breakfast on the Day itself when the gifts from Santa had been played with but before the huge pile of presents under the tree were attacked.

As long as old Moses was alive, he was the one who cut the cedar from the pasture. Its smell permeated the house and its feathery branches enchanted each generation, hung as it was with more and more ornaments saved over the years from the generations before. Then Jesse took over the task and when he was too old, we searched the stores for a cedar tree but, alas, settled in the last years for spruce or pine. Lizzie Chalmers' velvet wreaths graced the windows when I was a child, fading from bright red to a pale salmon hue when my children were small. Peeking at the presents under the tree and prying loose the end of a wrapping began with the Chalmers children, then beckoning Novice and Bubba, continuing as Wilson and Mary Elizabeth sneaked a look in the twenties. My cousin Barbara coaxed me (with little effort) into the game in the fifties. I caught my twins, encouraged by their brothers, doing the same one Christmas Eve in the 1970's. We gazed at the ornaments, most of them very old, with wonder. Our favorite were the "Bubble lights." Probably dating from the early nineteen hundreds, they were magical and a bit scary. Shaped like a candle with a cup of water in a base of each, the heat in the water began to bubble up, causing the candle to bubble with continuous movement. We were fascinated and waited for the water to be heated by the ancient electric wires, heavy and thick, covered in cloth, plugged into the wall. Possibly a fire hazard by the sixties, Mother sadly disposed of them.

Two years before Mother's death, she had grown tired and fragile and had much of the meal brought in by caterers. She hired a dear gentleman, Theodore, to serve the feast on Christmas Eve. He appeared with silver trays in hand, white-gloved and smiling. My mother adored him. The next Christmas, in 2001, he was, himself, too old and not up to the task. Mother accepted our help, all the females in the family, in providing the meal. She ate at the table in her velvet dressing gown. Seated in a wheelchair, she thanked us tearfully, for "one more Christmas." She must have sensed that it would be her last.

Tiny Caroline, my first grandchild, was the last of the children to come down the stairs singing "Jingle Bells" on Christmas morning. It was 2005 and she toddled down, holding her stuffed dog 'Spot'. All of us, the entire family, gathered below to watch her. Filled with memories of our own Newberry Christmases, there was not a dry eye. She was the seventh generation.

The traditions of Christmases spent in the old home of our ancestors runs in our blood and permeates our memories. Lizza will say, "Oh! Smell that! It's a boxwood and it reminds of the walkway in Newberry!" Mark and John still love to dress for the formal dinner on Christmas Eve and insist on the same menu as 'Nano' served. Erin has mastered the macaroni and cheese dish that her grandmother made famous, a recipe passed to her from Lizzie Chalmers.

And we are so like them in ways large and small. There are the clear blue eyes of Jane Allen Sloan. The thin stature but strong constitution of her husband Thomas and the heart for God possessed by the Chalmers' and Browns'. The women in our family, some more than others, are all strong and determined, whip-smart like Lizzie and Liz but nurturing and sensitive like Novice. Our men are humorous and quick-witted. Some are wise like the extraordinary Wilson Brown and ambitious and driven like Harrison Moore. To be sure, the love of family and hearth and home has been bequeathed to us down through time by Thomas and Jane Chalmers as surely as their blood runs yet in our veins.

May it ever be.

Epilogue

September, 2008

We've come home to bury him. Our dear "Pop", as the grandchildren named him, inevitably lost his battle with the dementia that tore his mind apart for twenty years.

When we, his four children, found his care too much for us, he spent his last year in the memory-care wing of a bright, efficient assisted living facility in Florida. It didn't matter to him, as it did to his wife, that he die in the old home where he had lived out happy years with her. It didn't matter, nor did he know, that he was on planet earth. The small comforts of food, a soft pillow, a kind touch were his last unspoken requests. He died with no memory of ever being married, having children or serving in a world war. His last thoughts were most likely of his nurturing, mid-western mother.

His funeral was not as large as that of his wife's, the hometown girl who had moved away for her husband's career but never lost the dream of coming back to live out her life on the old land of her heritage. She had been, as her daughters' had called her, "the last of the great Southern Belles." Many in her town had grown up with her and had come to pay tribute at her wake. Laid out in the parlor where generations of her people had been thusly displayed in various velvet-lined coffins, she would have been pleased that this old tradition of the small town south was being accorded her. Visitors passed by her casket, admired her beautifully knitted suit and tasteful jewelry, then headed to the bar for a 'cordial.' Things were cordial indeed and the paying of respects, between sips of Bourbon, turned into jocularity and stories of the beauteous, impeccable Liz and her well-loved family.

"Shhh", warned my sister. "This is getting' kinda' loud. I don't hink they're used to doing things like this," she frowned.

"Oh, sure they are," countered sister number two in her sweet way. "Mama would love this." Indeed, she would have. Nothing pleased her more than a good party in her gracious home. And when someone whispered to me quietly referring to her as "the most beautiful corpse I've ever seen," she would have loved that too.

But years had passed since that January and most of Mother and Dad's friends had died or were infirm in some way. So this gathering for my father had been smaller. Very dignified, as he would have wanted, with his grandson receiving the folded American flag accorded a veteran in his honor, but smaller.

Later that evening, we sit around the den in our baggy jeans and bathrobes and talk of both of them. "Do you think Nano and Pop can see us?" my niece asks. She has the delicate skin of her Irish ancestry and bears the proud name of "Sloan."

"Maybe," Bunny answers. "Hope so. They're sorry they're not here drinking Scotch with us!" A laugh, now, from the group. The sadness is beginning to be assuaged by camaraderie and the bond of family love. Just the closeness and warmth of those who have always been a part of each other is soothing. Familiar eyes, voices we have always known. Even the comforting scent of those whose blood is our own.

"Do you think this house has ghosts?" asks my daughter. Some stifle a snicker, but those of us who have pondered such things think awhile.

"Well, the way I figure, at least fifteen people have either been born or died in this house," I offer. "I was the first to be born in a hospital, I know that."

"No way," my son says with honest astonishment.

"Yeah, didn't you know that? Granddaddy delivered me."

"Eeeeuuuww," a chorus of loud disgust issues forth followed by laughter. Funny how we think alike.

"Gross......how'd you like *your* Dad delivering your baby!" More laughter.

My husband quips, "Well, in the heat of the moment, the woman wouldn't give a darn!"

Lots of guffaws. Then John speaks up, "You said that just like Rhett Butler!"

"Y'all are too much for me," Sally says, "Pour me some more scotch."

"How did they-----, well, who delivered, you know, the babies back in the Civil war times?" Mark asks curiously.

"They let nature take its' course, I guess, and women helped each other. Of course, there were a lot of doctors in our own family."

"And I guess slaves helped their mistresses in the old days. Didn't most mistresses help their slave women, too?" Molly speaks up from under her iPod-plugged ears. "Anyway, that's what Scarlett's mama did in the movie."

"Oh, Lord, not more "Gone with the Wind!" someone chides. The room breaks up in mirth.

"Anyway," another cousin chimes in, "what about ghosts? Has anybody ever seen one here or heard anything, you know—banging and bumping in the night and all?"

"One night when I was staying with Dad," Bunny begins, "I kept turning on the lamp on the piano, the one we leave on at night, and it kept being turned off. Gave me the willies."

"Maybe it was Dad getting up and wanting it turned off. Maybe the bulb was loose and shorted out. I don't know if I believe stuff like that......," Sally says pensively. Her loss has deeply affected her. She was the apple of Dad's eye and, although the father we all knew had been gone for years in spirit, the physical loss cut deep.

My daughter then launches into a vivid description of mysterious doings at her job in an old civil war museum and event facility in Atlanta. "I'm not making this up, y'all". Elizabeth promises. "There was a picture of a Union soldier hanging on the wall in the same room with Confederate guys and, without fail, the Yankee's picture would be on the floor every morning when the first person got to work. It became a joke. Then one night I had to work late and strange things happened."

"Like what?" This from her twin sister Erin who had most likely heard this story but is setting the stage for the finale. No drama was ever lost on these two.

The room grows silent and I slip out, intent on finding a cotton robe I had brought. I know Elizabeth is telling her tale of doors slamming and footsteps in hallways. She would never make anything up. Her truthfulness is legendary. The air of late summer is still pleasant but I feel unusually warm in the room with all of us gathered about.

I pass by the portraits of possible ghosts and give them a wink. I'd kind of like it if one of them would make him or herself known to us. I vow anew to do some research on the personalities who have occupied these rooms over the century and a half since the building of the first log cabin-----the very room where my family sits, laughingly talking of ghosts.

Back downstairs, I anticipate closing the heavy double doors to the porch as the night grows darker. But something makes me want to go outside. I sit for a moment, still able to hear the ghost-talk from the front room. The night is still sweet with the perfume of gardenias and the last of summer honeysuckle. I lean against a tall column and notice its paint beginning to peel. It will be up to us now, the siblings, who must see to the upkeep until one of us, if at all possible, should decide to move to the small town and repeat the tradition of making the farm, called "Greenfield' since the 1970's, our home.

Crickets chirp and a whippoorwill, some distance away, begins his nightly sonata. Memories of childhood flood my senses. The sounds and smells of late summer in the countryside are part of my flesh as surely as those who jostle and cajole each other in the next room. I know that, very late, a bobolink in the pasture will chime in with his plaintive call. Have they always been there, maybe for centuries, a family of late-night singers? Did the Chalmers forefathers, in this same house, hear such tuneful reverie from one tiny creature?

"Hey, guys, y'all need to come out here on the porch. It's cooler and there are a million stars." Before I finish the sentence, bodies start drifting out. Some lounge on the enormous stone steps, others fill up wicker and rocking chairs. For a moment, no one speaks. They are drinking it all in, the perfumed night, the cloudless firmament, a symphony of pastoral sounds both near this place we call home and far away down the roads and in the fields.

Glasses tinkle with cocktail ice. Sons and daughters of Liz and Joe, of the Browns and Sloans and Chalmers, relax on the sturdy, broad-beamed porch our ancestors built. There is tranquility in the fresh country air, our individual, unspoken pain salved by the velvet night. Brown eyed Joseph, his grandfather's namesake asks, "What will become of all this?"

Bunny, second of the siblings, is quiet. Closest to mother and dad in these last years, she has never had children. Her aging parents, seeing to their lives as they aged, was her calling. She sips her drink as she gazes out over the acres in the moonlight. Many miles away, easily heard across the flat plains of the Carolina Piedmont, the low roll of thunder promises the first of autumn's rains. A silver tear slides down my sister's cheek.

There is no answer, at least not on this night, not so soon. If those who have gone before us know the answer, we will know too, in time. On this night it is enough just to be here, in this fine place, with each other.

References

- John Belton Oneill, <u>The Annals of Newberry, Vols.I and II</u>
- Charles Edward Cauthen and Tracy Power, <u>South Carolina Goes to War,1860-1865,</u>
- E.L. Doctorow, <u>The March</u>
- David Nevin and Time-Life Books, <u>Sherman's March: Atlanta to the Sea</u>
- Ted Banta, Executive Director of The South Carolina Battleground Preservation Trust, Inc. <u>"Bloody Bridge" or "The Battle for Burden's Causeway"</u>
- Edward Ball, <u>Slaves In The Family</u>
- John Andrew Creasy, Jr., <u>Watters/Moore</u>
- John Andrew Creasy, Jr., <u>Joseph. S. Watters and the 494th Bombardment Group</u>
- John Rigdon, <u>Sherman's March Through South Carolina</u>
- James Alvin Brown and Jane Brown Bunn, <u>Simms Brown Family 1750-1981</u>
- John Andrew Creasy, Jr., <u>Reminiscences of A Southern Childhood: A Memoir of Mary Elizabeth Watters (1920-2002)</u>
- Dr. Wilson Caldwell Brown, <u>The History Of Mt. Bethel Academy</u>
- <u>Family Bible- King James Version</u>, notations made by Jane Allen Sloan Chalmers
- <u>United States Census, 1850-1930</u>, Archived from the original, June, 2010.

Acknowlegdements

The author wishes to thank Mrs. Grier Kimbrell MacFarland of Vero Beach, Florida, historian and genealogist, for her extensive research of the Sloan, Thompson, Chalmers and Brown families.

A special thankyou to Mrs. Charlotte Wolf for her expert proofreading and exhaustive hours spent in helping to edit this book.

Author's note: As of the completion of this book, the fate of the old Sloan-Chalmers home has been determined. As no family member could see their way clear to move into the dwelling of our heritage, it was decided the house should be sold. This took place in 2013, the purchaser being, ironically, another doctor—and a female doctor at that. It is our hope that her own grandchildren may play in the backyard under the old pecan trees as so many generations of our family have done. It tore our hearts to see this legacy pass from our hands, but we rejoice that it will escape the destruction of so many glorious treasures that dot the by-ways of the South, as was fate of the majestic plantation belonging to Col. J.C.S. Brown.

"To everything there is season and a time to every purpose under the heaven……A time to get and a time to lose; a time to keep and a time to cast away." Ecclesiastes 3

Engagement picture: Mary Elizabeth Moore and Lt. Joseph Skead Watters 1943

The Brown family, around 1910
Lizzie. Wilson, Chalmers (Bubba) and Novice

Colonel John Christopher Sims Brown, Pappy's father, around 1905
1831-1910

Colonel J.C.S. Brown, Dr. Wilson Brown, Lizzie Brown
Around 1909

Pappy riding "Ranger", about 1910

Mary Elizabeth and her brother Wilson, about 1923

Joseph Watters (far right), with his twin sister Sally and brother Albert
Shelby, Ohio, around 1925

Laurie and Bunny Watters, off to school, Atlanta, 1954

Liz and Joe, surrounded by their Children and Grandchildren,
On the occasion of their 50th wedding anniversary.
Bermuda, September, 1993

The author, Laurie Watters Shoemaker, with the seventh generation, 2015
Harrison, Caroline, Jack and Mary Claire